About Island Press

Since 1984, the nonprofit organization Island Press has been stimulating, shaping, and communicating ideas that are essential for solving environmental problems worldwide. With more than 1,000 titles in print and some 30 new releases each year, we are the nation's leading publisher on environmental issues. We identify innovative thinkers and emerging trends in the environmental field. We work with world-renowned experts and authors to develop cross-disciplinary solutions to environmental challenges.

Island Press designs and executes educational campaigns, in conjunction with our authors, to communicate their critical messages in print, in person, and online using the latest technologies, innovative programs, and the media. Our goal is to reach targeted audiences—scientists, policy makers, environmental advocates, urban planners, the media, and concerned citizens—with information that can be used to create the framework for long-term ecological health and human well-being.

Island Press gratefully acknowledges major support from The Bobolink Foundation, Caldera Foundation, The Curtis and Edith Munson Foundation, The Forrest C. and Frances H. Lattner Foundation, The JPB Foundation, The Kresge Foundation, The Summit Charitable Foundation, Inc., and many other generous organizations and individuals.

The opinions expressed in this book are those of the author(s) and do not necessarily reflect the views of our supporters.

CURBING TRAFFIC

Curbing Traffic

The Human Case for
Fewer Cars in Our Lives

Melissa Bruntlett and
Chris Bruntlett

ISLANDPRESS | Washington | Covelo

Library of Congress Control Number: 2020946213

All Island Press books are printed on environmentally responsible materials.

Manufactured in the United States of America
10 9 8 7 6 5 4 3 2 1

Keywords: Access to nature, aging in place, childhood autonomy, climate
resilience, cycling city, Delft, "low-car" city, mental health, mobility choice,
the Netherlands, noise pollution, protected bike lane, street design,
traffic calming, transportation accessibility

MIX
Paper from
responsible sources
FSC
www.fsc.org   FSC® C008955

For Wendy, Ed, Margaret, and Robert,
our biggest fans and
most ardent supporters.

Our story has only been possible
because of your unwavering encouragement,
no matter where our journey has taken us.

Contents

Introduction

Living the "Low-Car" City

I t was only supposed to be five blog posts. But when our family first traveled from Vancouver to Rotterdam in the summer of 2016, we had no idea how quickly a simple writing assignment would spiral out of control. Those five online articles would form the basis for our book *Building the Cycling City: The Dutch Blueprint for Urban Vitality*, whose publication by Island Press in August 2018 transformed these two Canadians into inadvertent international ambassadors for the Netherlands. Focused on the forward-thinking urban and transport planning policies that have transformed Dutch cities from places for cars to places for people, the book also provided concrete case studies of North American communities already translating these concepts onto their streets. Following a global speaking tour that saw us address 44 audiences in 25 cities across seven countries (including a once-in-a-lifetime trip across Australia and New Zealand), and countless media appearances—such as Vox, *The Guardian*, CityLab, National Public Radio, and the Canadian Broadcasting Corporation—we returned home to the Pacific Northwest with a life-changing decision to make. But to be honest, it was a fairly easy one.

After featuring Dutch Cycling Embassy (former) director Mirjam Borsboom in a chapter of *Building the Cycling City*, and then meeting Mobycon CEO Johan Diepens at our Ottawa book launch, the process of writing and promoting our first book became one gigantic job interview. And sure enough, in early 2019, the two of us were staring at employment offers from these respective organizations, both located in the small city of Delft: Melissa as international communications specialist for Mobycon, and Chris as marketing and communication manager for the Dutch Cycling Embassy. So, with very little hesitation, we reduced all of our earthly belongings into eight suitcases (and a cat carrier), pulled the children out of school midsemester, and traded the peaks of British Columbia for the lowlands of South Holland, eager to begin exporting the inspiring bicycle infrastructure and culture we'd been fervently touting for years.

Aside from it being the home of the eponymous *Delfts blauw* (Delft blue) pottery, the birthplace of Johannes Vermeer, and the assassination site of Willem van Oranje, (the main leader of the sixteenth-century Dutch Revolt against the Spanish Habsburgs), we knew precious little about our new hometown. We had not even set foot there until we arrived at the door of our rental apartment on a February morning in 2019. It was love at first sight, and within hours of wandering its quaint canals, cobbled streets, and historic squares, it became clear that we had—as one of our Twitter followers so eloquently put it—"met onze neus in de boter gevallen" (fallen with our nose in the butter). This was an immense relief, as we had initially considered settling in some of the surrounding cities, but with both of our jobs located within a short cycle ride, it made sense to stay close to the kids as they transitioned into the public-school system. Coralie and Etienne, at the ages of 12 and 10 respectively, were understandably a bit more hesitant about this intercontinental move. But despite its being our warm and welcoming home for 11 wonderful years, all four of us were ready to "downsize" from big and bustling Vancouver, and Delft seemed to check all of our boxes: a compact and historic college town of just over 100,000 people—30,000 of whom study or work at the local university—where an incredible four-fifths of all journeys are made on foot, bicycle, or public transport (and no less than half of all trips are on a bicycle!).

In addition to the obvious (and ongoing) adjustment to a new language and culture, the starkest discovery was the myriad qualitative benefits that come with living in a place with far fewer motor vehicles. Even with high expectations, the first few weeks were nothing short of a revelation for our family; each day discovering the immense joys of living in a city that treated cars as guests, rather than guests of honor. Suddenly we found ourselves living in an environment where we could

Our multimodal family savoring the joy and freedom of movement discovered in "low-car" Delft. From right to left: Etienne, Chris, Melissa, and Coralie. (Marijn Diepens)

hear again. Having been accustomed to the prevalence of engines, we had forgotten the sounds that give life to a city: people talking, birds singing, bells ringing, and music playing. At the same time, we watched our children enjoy the independence and freedom of moving autonomously on their own streets. These inclusive spaces welcomed virtually anyone; including the aging and disabled. In this immersive environment, levels of trust and compassion were clear through eye contact with fellow travelers. We saw how such an environment permits frequent and meaningful connections with our community, allowing us to meet and interact with our new neighbors.

Beyond the physical reaction to how it felt to move through Delft, we discovered new psychological and sociological benefits we hadn't anticipated. The stress, frustration, and anxiety that had been an assumed part of our daily travels around Vancouver had all but disappeared. Feelings of isolation were soon replaced with a sense of belonging to this city, as we interacted with our fellow residents on its footpaths, streets, and cycle tracks. And improved social equity—at least in the public realm—was not a question but a reality. As we traveled throughout Delft, the divisions between age, gender, race, and class were far less distinguishable. Regardless of where we went, we crossed paths with Delft's diverse demographic groups: the young and old, individuals across the economic spectrum, people of color, and those living with disabilities. In our eyes, virtually everyone was afforded the same respect and dignity of autonomously transporting themselves from A to B.

As we started sharing these observations on social media, we eventually came to the realization that, despite writing an entire book on the topic, "The Dutch Blueprint for Urban Vitality" isn't really about bicycles. It's about refusing to sacrifice vast amounts of the public realm to the private automobile; instead reserving space for commerce, community, and social connection. The ubiquitous bicycles are simply a by-product of that larger process; a tool to achieve the end goal of what policy makers call an *autoluw* (low-car or nearly car-free) city. At the same time, while we had been so focused on communicating the myriad benefits of cycling, it became clear that although not the stated intention of these transport policies, the improvements to social and emotional well-being resulting from decisions play—rather discreetly—a huge role in improving the livability of cities.

In going back through the archives and history of our adopted hometown, as well as "learning on the job" through our respective jobs, we were pleasantly surprised to learn that Delft was on the leading edge of that "traffic evaporation" trend that began five decades ago in the Netherlands. Around that time, a culture of innovation and experimentation at Delft City Hall created a willingness to try new things (and sometimes even fail); ultimately changing the way cities across the country approach motor traffic circulation, residential street design, and bicycle network planning, and providing the inspiration for global cities to do the same.

Delft is a fairly small city, and would be easy to dismiss when discussing the challenges of larger regions like Los Angeles, London, or Melbourne. But its successes must be viewed in—and wouldn't be possible without—the greater context of the Randstad (Rim City).

A circular-shaped megalopolis, the Randstad is made up of 22 cities (including the Netherlands' four largest: Amsterdam, Rotterdam, The Hague, and Utrecht), Europe's largest port (Rotterdam) and third busiest airport (Schiphol), and 8.2 million residents. Delft's proximity (around 10 kilometers, or 6 miles) to the centers of both Rotterdam and The Hague makes it ostensibly a suburb of each city, complete with convenient light/heavy rail and bicycle access. In that context, Delft is to the Randstad what Santa Monica is to Los Angeles, Tottenham is to London, or Yarra is to Melbourne. Or for that matter, what our former neighborhood of Grandview-Woodland is to the Greater Vancouver metropolitan area.

Vancouver is a city that will forever remain near and dear to our hearts, and one that has made tremendous strides in sustainable transport in the past decade, with two-thirds of all trips now made by foot, bicycle, or public transport. But like Delft, its successes must be viewed in the larger context of the Greater Vancouver metropolitan area. The city of Vancouver, for example, is just a single 115-square-kilometer (44-square-mile) municipality of 675,000 residents within a sprawling 2,877-square-kilometer (1,110-square-mile) region of 23 local authorities and over 2.5 million people. The impressive statistics cited include only trips beginning and ending within city limits, and exclude the nearly three-quarters of regional journeys that take place in an automobile. Hundreds of thousands of cars pass in and out of the city each day. These vehicles are not traveling on elevated highways (to its credit, Vancouver is the only major North American city without one), but on residential streets retrofitted into at-grade arterial roads that bisect its various communities, shifting the resulting externalities (air pollution, noise pollution, traffic collisions, reduced livability, etc.) from the outer suburbs onto the inner city. Furthermore, with practically all of the municipality's energy focused on the downtown peninsula and affluent western neighborhoods, many other areas, arguably the ones most in need of investments in safer streets—due to higher active travel use and lower incomes—were regularly left out in the cold.

We were able to better quantify and comprehend our dramatic increase in quality of life several months after landing in Delft, and accessing the City of Vancouver's traffic counts for our former neighborhood of Grandview-Woodland. We were shocked to learn that a staggering 150,000 cars moved within 100 meters (328 feet) of our East Vancouver apartment each day, with the vast majority exceeding the posted speed limit of 50 km/h (30 mph). In comparison, in our current home in Hof van Delft, just outside the city center, barely 1,500 cars pass within 100 meters each day; the vast majority no faster than 30 km/h (20 mph). Having far fewer cars in our lives brought obvious and not-so-obvious benefits to each member of our family, from lower exposure to air and noise pollution, to reduction of chronic stress, an increase in physical activity, and feelings of social connectivity.

"First we shape our cities, and then they shape us," wrote Jan Gehl in 2010, paraphrasing Sir Winston Churchill, who at the time, was referring to the unique ability of the architect to influence and improve society. Gehl's update reflects a mounting realization among planners, politicians, and policy makers that it's not so much our buildings that shape us, as Churchill had insisted, but the space between them. This space has the potential to increase the autonomy and freedom of children; improve sociability and trust between citizens; create more gender, age, and ability-equitable spaces; improve access to opportunity to all citizens; and ultimately create a city more resilient to the stresses of the present and future.

In most Western countries, since the Second World War, this public space has been monopolized and dominated by the private automobile. Recent years have seen an unprecedented push for a more equitable reallocation of this (curb and street) space—especially for walking and cycling—in metropolitan areas across the globe. Fueled by converging climate, health, and safety crises, there is a growing urgency to reduce the speed, access, and volume of cars, in residential and commercial areas alike. The COVID-19 pandemic has further fueled this challenge to the hegemony of cars in cities, as physical distancing requirements suddenly forced citizens to question this inefficient allowance of space. But by focusing on facts, figures, and charts, these discussions often miss the most critical element: the human one.

In the following chapters, the story of our first two years in Delft provides the backdrop for how this city, and many others like it in the Netherlands, ultimately succeeded in creating more human spaces.

Looking beyond transport planning, policy, and design, we examine the growing body of research into the social and psychological impacts of automobile domination, including what happens when we start to reduce their prevalence, both from our streets and from our lives. The city we now call home does not exist in a bubble, and in reality, reflects many others across the globe. If *Building the Cycling City* offers the blueprint for *how* to create urban vitality, *Curbing Traffic* provides the reasons *why* cities and towns designed for people are so important for our individual and societal health and well-being.

In attempting to describe our new lives in Delft to the outside world, we find ourselves regularly returning to an analogy authored by Edinburgh-based blogger Robert Weetman in a 2017 post. He theorizes the experience of visiting the Netherlands for the first time through the eyes of someone who has spent their entire life standing in a cloud of flies. Life is possible, but the flies are omnipresent. The person can breathe, but they have to wear a mask. They can see, but they have to brush flies out their eyes to do so. They can hear, but they have to strain to listen. They can stay fairly healthy, but the flies make it harder to do so. Now imagine stepping into a world where those flies have mostly disappeared. Weetman's apt analogy is no longer hypothetical for our family; it is our day-to-day reality. We navigate Delft's streets with our senses engaged, seemingly for the first time. And it is something we believe the entire world deserves to experience firsthand.

Chapter 1

The Child-Friendly City

Our culture obsesses about the care of children. We declare their well-being the most important thing in the world. Yet we keep building places that steal their freedom and put them in danger. I often wonder, "What kind of place would we create if we really wanted to meet our stated ambition of caring for children?"
— Charles Montgomery

"If you're going to live here, then you're going to have to get used to riding a bike." These words, uttered by an emergency room nurse at the Reinier de Graaf Hospital in Delft, might be the most vivid memory of our family's first few months on Dutch soil. It was an evening in April 2019, barely seven weeks since we had crossed the Atlantic to start our new lives in the Netherlands. Our son Etienne, we would soon discover, had suffered a slight fracture in the humerus bone of his left arm, after tumbling from his bicycle on his way home from school that afternoon.

What the nurse didn't know is that Etienne, at the tender age of 10, had already been cycling confidently for the better part of six years, riding in dozens of cities—and all kinds of conditions—across North America, Europe, and Australasia. The irony that it took moving to *fietsparadijs* (bicycle paradise) for one of our kids to have their first broken bone was not lost on us, and makes us chuckle to this day.

It makes perfect sense, though. Nearly two months of riding around Delft independently had created a sense of ease and complacency in Etienne, causing him to momentarily let his guard down; something his classmates likely experienced from time to time. Pedaling along a main thoroughfare—Voorhofdreef—on the segregated cycle track, which was 3 meters (10 feet) wide and many meters from the nearest automobile, he simply lost his concentration, took a spill, and experienced what the Dutch call an *eenzijdig ongeluk* (one-sided accident). Thankfully, due to the forgiving nature of the street design, no pedestrian, bicycle, or motor vehicle was involved, and he was lucky enough to walk away from the incident without any life-threatening or life-changing injuries.

While the nurse proceeded to wrap Etienne's arm in a plaster cast, she quizzed us about our decision to relocate to Delft. Like countless others we had spoken to in those first few weeks, she couldn't comprehend why anyone would choose to give up the expansive and stunning natural beauty of Canada for her tiny, monotonous, and cramped country. So, for seemingly the dozenth time since landing at Schiphol Airport, we explained that—at its core—this move was about our children. We wanted to offer them the same liberation and self-determination experienced by most Dutch children (without their even knowing it). This is something we had longed to be able to provide them in Canada, but the built environment did not support or facilitate their needs. What surprised us, however, was how quickly they adapted to—and even reveled in—their newly discovered autonomy in the Netherlands.

Etienne's new elementary school was 3 kilometers (2 miles) south of our apartment; a 15-minute bike ride at his lackadaisical pace. After our accompanying him each way for a couple of weeks, one day he simply decided he could make it home without Mom or Dad, and never looked back. Now he regularly walks into the city center to raid the candy store, pedals to art class at the public library, and even makes the lengthy trip to the neighboring city of Rijswijk to visit his friend, riding the 7 kilometers (4 miles) unaccompanied. Even with his arm in a cast—and unable to cycle for five weeks—he quickly adapted, taking advantage of his *OV-chipkaart* (public transport pass) and the local tram network, which conveniently dropped him off within a short distance of most destinations in his little world.

At the same time, 13-year-old Coralie, dropped into her first year of high school, immediately set off without intervention to discover her

Etienne's first school commute in the Netherlands. During the morning rush hour, the cycle tracks on Voorhofdreef are bustling with parents and kids alike. (Modacity)

own way of getting from A to B (and C and D). Notorious for being directionally challenged—as evidenced by one or two bus rides in the wrong direction in Vancouver—she was suddenly more confident in figuring out her routes, and even okay with getting lost once in a while.

Much like we hoped and dreamed, our teenage daughter joined the hordes of adolescents walking and cycling around Delft, completely void of "annoying" parental supervision. Her confidence inspired us to continue letting go, culminating in her making the three-hour, 240-kilometer (150-mile) train trip north, by herself, to visit a friend in Groningen for the weekend. After proving her capabilities on the streets of Delft, she gave us confidence that she had the skills and knowledge to manage the journey on her own; and if something did go awry, we were just a quick phone call away.

For most people born and raised in this country, like the emergency room nurse, the degree of self-sufficiency among children is completely underappreciated. Like most fish have no clue they're surrounded by water, the vast majority of Dutch people have little understanding of the remarkable ways their cities have been shaped to make them more secure, inclusive, and pleasant for all ages. As is so often the case, it takes an outsider to hold up a proverbial mirror, and share their experiences of joy and wonder, for locals to truly appreciate what they've accomplished.

The stark contrast from our Canadian experience left us wondering: besides the obvious factors—ample cycle tracks and traffic-calmed streets—what was facilitating such different attitudes and experiences? What exactly did it mean for the well-being of our children, and what were their peers elsewhere missing out on?

Raising the Backseat Generation

For as long as humans have been living in cities, and until only recently, streets were the main site where children grew up. With larger families the norm until the 1960s, kids were pushed outside, leaving mothers to manage their daily activities free from the bother of their offspring. With all of the neighborhood children outside playing together, the community took responsibility for their welfare. Neighbors kept a watchful eye on each other's little ones, and shop owners on those mixed-purpose streets were familiar with their faces. By and large, however, there was a general understanding: children largely had the capacity to manage themselves.

Dr. Lia Karsten, associate professor of urban geography at the University of Amsterdam, defines this group as outdoor children—children who played outside every day, and ultimately claimed the streets for their own. In the decades to come, however, two new categories of childhood emerged. As fast-moving and parked cars along these neighborhood streets increased, the children's play space was lost, and the kids were pushed elsewhere. "The public space of the street used to be a child space, but it has been transformed to an adult space," Karsten explains. Inversely, the private home evolved from a place for adults into one belonging to children.

"Now that outdoor children have grown into a small minority, nowadays, geographical childhood can be classified mainly into two types:

namely 'indoor children' and children of the 'backseat generation,'" says Karsten. Indoor children rarely play outside, and when they do, it is for short periods of time. The act of play becomes much more of an indoor activity, frequently involving an electronic screen. They are typically lower-class kids living in car-dominated neighborhoods, without the means to fill their free time with programmed pursuits. These children and their parents report feelings of anxiousness related to the idea of being outside.

Dr. Karsten defines the Achterbankgeneratie (backseat generation) as those children who are escorted everywhere and "whose time-space behavior is characterized primarily by adult-organized activities." They are largely middle- and upper-class kids who are chauffeured from home to school, from sports practice to the museum, and from the cinema to music lessons. But whether *indoor* or *backseat*, the cause is the same: lack of safety and space due to a rise in the number of cars.

"Children and cars are competitors," Karsten states definitively, "because cars occupy the street and the space in front of the house. What we see is parents are more afraid because of the danger of motorized traffic. This danger is directly in front of the house, which should be one of the safest places for children." An age group that was once thought of as resilient is now treated as vulnerable; in need of constant management and supervision. Within a few generations, their ability to wander their streets has quickly diminished and, for many, completely disappeared.

With the lack of places to play—and ultimately move—kids and their activities are now pushed toward specially designated "safe" spaces. Think of the neighborhood park or playground, after-school programs, play-gyms, and community centers, the only places children now enjoy physical activity and social interaction. While these locations provide safety and comfort for both parents and their offspring, they ultimately set kids apart from the rest of society, in a sense defining them as "the other."

When this development is viewed from the perspective of the transport network, this means that the ability to roam independently is replaced with supervised movement, often from the backseat of the family automobile. These additional trips, in combination with traffic being allowed to race through their neighborhood streets, has turned the places that children often frequent into metaphorical "islands."

The City as an Archipelago

"The city is an archipelago consisting of different places of which their own street is only one island in a chain," explains Karsten. "They move—escorted—from one domain to another in their urban field, constructing their identities as modern young kids." Growing up in an environment where they fail to grasp how they progress from island to island, these children become completely reliant on adults for their navigation and transportation needs. For both indoor children and the backseat generation, their agency is reduced to the reach of their parents' eyesight.

This problematic concept of the city as an archipelago was later reinforced by Dr. Steven Fleming—an architect and the author of *Cycle Space* and *Velotopia*—who in 2017, began studying and mapping the consequences of street grids on walking and cycling rates in his hometown of Newcastle, Australia. When the effects of uncrossable arterial roads and rat running (the practice of using residential side streets or any other unintended shortcut) motorists were visualized on a map, Fleming concluded that most city dwellers were effectively living on islands.

"To a risk averse cyclist, a child for example, the city would feel like a hundred small islands with what might as well be oceans between them," Fleming observed. "Arterial roads with limited safe crossing opportunities for people, and residential streets engineered to provide drivers with shortcuts leave most cyclists trapped on the street where they live. How can they access school, jobs, or shops?"

This perfectly captures our family's own experiences in East Vanouver. Despite living in a neighborhood with some of the lowest rates of car usage and ownership, and the highest rates of active travel in the region, we found ourselves surrounded on all four sides by four- and six-lane arterial roads that each carried upward of 40,000 vehicles per day; a huge number of which were just passing through. To make

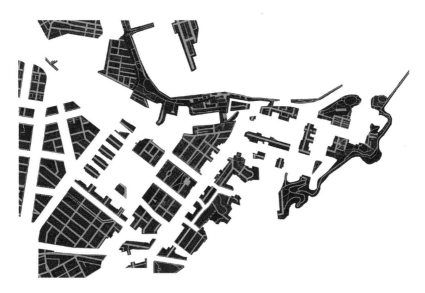

When mapping the impact of arterial roads in Newcastle, Australia, Dr. Fleming found most city dwellers were effectively living on islands. (Steven Fleming and Ben Thorp)

matters worse, Commercial Drive—the vibrant high street where we did all of our local shopping, dining, and after-school activities—had the dual and conflicting function of serving as a four-lane arterial road that moved 20,000 cars per day. Not only did this negatively impact our health, happiness, and mobility, but it also limited the ability of our children to walk or cycle a few blocks to their school, the local community center, or a friend's house without Mom or Dad by their side.

Furthermore, every single street design element prioritized passing cars over people who lived in our community. Faded, unraised, and poorly lit crosswalks made traversing the street a game of Russian roulette; the outcome resting in the hands of motorists racing from one red light to the next. Where driveways and alleyways intersected with sidewalks, the footpath completely disappeared, leaving pedestrians trespassing in "no man's land." Then there were the "beg buttons"—the devices used by pedestrians to request permission to cross the street—at controlled crossings, located mere inches from cars whizzing by at 80 km/h (50 mph). Considering how the deck was stacked, few could fault parents insisting on shuttling kids from place to place, instead of letting them use their own two feet.

According to Karsten, greater supervision of play and movement has an obvious influence on a child's ability to exist independently. Even in the Netherlands, a great deal of supervised mobility occurs— albeit by bicycle—until the child is 9 or 10, creating a backseat generation of sorts. But she is quick to point out that there are some positive benefits to these trends. Increased parental participation in children's lives equates to a stronger child–parent bond, where the child is viewed less as a burden and more as a contributing member of the family. But with declining levels of social cohesion, physical activity, and unstructured play in almost every neighborhood, it is difficult to argue that these benefits outweigh the drawbacks.

A Drop in Active and Independent Travel

The first, and most obvious, impact of the backseat generation is the reduction in the rates of physical activity—and overall health—of children. A staggering 93 percent of Canadian kids and 80 percent of American kids do not get the recommended hour of daily physical activity. One in three Canadian children are either overweight or obese, a vicious cycle that proves difficult to break as they enter adulthood. By 2040, almost three-quarters of Canadian adults will be overweight, significantly increasing their risk of heart disease, cancer, stroke, type 2 diabetes, and costing the health care system over C$100 billion per year. Sadly, this generation of children could be the first in the history of Western civilization to live less healthful and shorter lives than their parents.

This generational drop in active and independent travel isn't unique to Canada. In 1971, 86 percent of British primary school children were allowed to travel home from school on their own. In 2010, it was 25 percent. In 1969, 50 percent of American kids walked or cycled to school. By 2009, that had dropped to just 13 percent. The number of parents ferrying their kids to school in a minivan or SUV (ironically, because they fear there are too many cars on the street) also contributes to growing congestion rates. A 2008 report from the New Zealand Department of

Transport estimated that up to a third of all automobiles on Auckland's roads during morning rush hour were parents dropping their children off at school. Currently, about two-thirds of all Dutch children walk or bike to school, with 75 percent of secondary school students cycling to school. By enabling safe and active travel, Dutch cities prevent an estimated one million car journeys to school each morning.

Then there is the growing link between active travel and academic performance, corroborated by a 2012 study of 20,000 Danish children between the ages of 5 and 19. It concluded that kids who cycled or walked to school, rather than being bussed or driven, performed better on tasks that required concentration—such as solving puzzles—and these effects lasted for up to four hours after they arrived.

The Diminishing Social Realm

Along with these mounting concerns about the sedentary lifestyle of the backseat generation, there is also a serious worry about their diminishing social capital. When streets were seen as places for children to gather and interact with peers, there were seemingly limitless opportunities to connect face-to-face with a diverse spectrum of peers from a wide variety of backgrounds. "On the level of the street, the integrated and intergenerational use of space was striking," suggests Karsten.

Today, as communities and schools become increasingly segregated, and play more prescribed, the chances to meet people unlike ourselves are decreasing dramatically. "While the street is declining in significance, the segregation among different class children is growing," Karsten says. In her research, she found that in migrant communities, residents agree that there is not enough space for children, stressing a lack of social safety: "With the growing diversity among neighbors, social contact and social control have faded away." In a Dutch context, migrant parents see it as problematic that their children cannot socialize with "native born" children, an important stage in acclimating and learning about local culture, while also sharing their own traditions and enriching the experiences of everyone involved.

This lack of integration has a dramatic effect on the social well-being of all children. With getting outside becoming a much less spontaneous act, kids have fewer chances to create new bonds with those outside their scheduled lives and existing social circles, leading to greater levels of isolation and loneliness. This isolation is particularly devastating to childhood development. For example, 5 to 10 percent of American kids under 18 are diagnosed with depression, with researchers finding a direct link between their physical inactivity and levels of loneliness leading to depression. This will have a lasting impact on their lives.

Social relationships are seen as critical to the maintenance of health, and a lack of them often correlates with feelings of loneliness. Loneliness, in turn, is linked to higher levels of stress. As it relates to children, that active stress response over an extended period of time is proven to increase the risk of developing cardiovascular disease, elevated blood pressure, infectious illness, cognitive deterioration, and mortality. By building cities in which their freedom of movement is restricted, the resulting social isolation has lasting effects on their physical and mental well-being.

But what about those children who experience frequent opportunities for social interaction, even when scheduled? While they may experience marginally lower levels of isolation, one thing is distinctly missing from play prescribed and supervised by parents that is integral to the development of a young mind: *risk*.

Raising the Bubble-Wrap Generation

Many parents can jovially recall days spent frolicking with their friends through the streets of their old neighborhood, perhaps going to places their own parents had warned were "out-of-bounds" and partaking in unsafe play. Maybe their adventures ended up being completely harmless or resulted in only a minor injury. But being deemed resilient enough to bounce back from minor setbacks, children were provided the opportunity to assess the risk, potentially make a mistake, and learn something along the way.

Many of today's children are so heavily supervised, and thought of as so vulnerable, that virtually all risk is removed from their day-to-day lives. "Dealing with risk is no longer seen as a part of growing up," laments Karsten. Missed opportunities for kids to evaluate danger are now being linked to poor coping strategies for dealing with adversity as they grow older; some university administrators have even referred to first-year students as "teacups." While it may be an amusing nickname for an entire cohort of young people (see also "bubble-wrap generation"), it is an indictment of how many parents have removed the tasks that would otherwise improve kids' ability to accurately assess and address risk. "After literally a lifetime of overprotection, these young adults are overwhelmed by sudden independence," writes Lenore Skenazy in the bestselling book *Free-Range Kids*. As a society, we have accepted this widespread tendency to overparent and overprotect such that we now subcategorize those who avoid this trap as an emerging trend. What Americans might call "free-range parenting," the Dutch simply call "parenting."

Even children's sleep habits are affected by our increasingly car-dominated transportation networks. For teenagers in particular, the backseat generation, and its lengthy travel times, presents a significant challenge. By creating communities that require driving to and from school— by either a parent, colleague, or bus—the health of kids between the ages of 10 and 18 is being severely neglected.

An increasing amount of research is emerging that shows teenagers require on average 8 to 10 hours of sleep each night. At the same time, their physiological clock is adjusting during their teen years, which demands later sleeping times. This is a constant for any generation. However, today's adolescents also need to contend with combining those biological sleep patterns with increasingly long commutes to school. Where just two or three generations ago, children would live near their secondary school, getting there by foot or bike, more students are traveling farther and farther distances by car, especially with the consolidation of high schools in the United States, and more specialized educational institutions elsewhere in the world.

According to a 2017 paper published in the *Journal of Planning Education and Research*, long commutes to school have direct negative impacts on children's well-being, especially on sleep and exercise. Traveling by car for upward of 30 minutes each morning and afternoon decreases the amount of time those students have to dedicate to getting exercise, leading to a significant decline of their physical health.

In relation to getting a good night's rest, for each additional minute a teenager spends commuting to school, they experience a 1.3-minute reduction in sleep time. Put into context, a student who travels 30 minutes to school sleeps 26 minutes less each night than a student who travels only 10 minutes. That loss of sleep can be linked to poor academic performance, unhealthy eating habits, and higher rates of obesity, as well as increased risks of depression due to greater stress.

Sadly, most teenagers spend their prime years dependent on others for their transport needs; counting down the days until they qualify for a driver's license. Dutch teens, conversely, spend those years experiencing the freedom and autonomy promised by the car, without its added stress, danger, and expense. Adolescents in the Netherlands regularly rank among the healthiest and happiest—with the lowest rates of obesity and antidepressant usage—on Earth. They also cycle, on average, an astonishing 2,000 kilometers (1,250 miles) per year. This is not a coincidence.

Exposure to Spatial Diversity

Experiencing the world from the backseat has one other detrimental psychological effect on children: they have little idea where they're going. As Dr. Bruce Appleyard discovered while studying two suburban neighborhoods in the San Francisco Bay Area in 2016, there is a direct correlation with the amount of time a child spends in a car, and the perception and understanding of their home territory.

When asked to draw a map of their community, children who were driven everywhere by their parents were unable to accurately depict how their streets connected. Rather, their illustrations showed a series of amorphous blobs—or "islands"—that represented their home, school, friends, or the mall, with little to no detail provided along the corridors between those nodes. On the other hand, children who predominantly got around their city on foot or bicycle were able to produce complex, highly detailed, and accurate maps of their neighborhood streets.

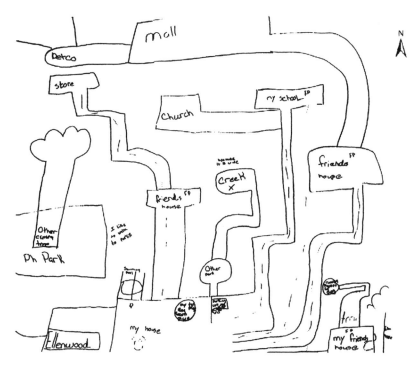

When asked to draw a map of their community, children who were driven everywhere couldn't accurately depict how their streets connected. (Bruce Appleyard)

We saw this up close and personal over the years, as we raised our children on two wheels in Vancouver. Quality time spent as a family was also quality time spent with our city, as the kids learned its streets like the backs of their hands. They knew all of the landmarks. They knew all of the neighborhoods. They knew all of the hills. They felt an intimacy with their city that they probably wouldn't have experienced had we been shuttling them around in car seats, as was the case for many of their peers.

We are doing our children no favors by creating urban environments that hand the entire public realm over to adults, particularly those privileged enough to travel around in a private automobile. At the same time, hearkening back to "the good old days" when kids used to play outside, minimizes the myriad obstacles that exist in the path to a better quality of life. So what can be done to give the streets back to young people and reinvigorate a new generation of *outdoor children*? As it turns out, the answer lies in the experiences of our own kids getting around Delft. And it's a strategy that can be being adapted to virtually any context, with the right political will.

Finding Freedom by Restricting Car Traffic

While much of Etienne and Coralie's newfound freedom could be attributed to the glorious red cycle tracks that crisscross Delft in every direction, we soon began to discover that even greater "invisible" forces were at play—forces that didn't just separate vulnerable road users from motorized vehicles but also removed as many of those vehicles from the urban environment as possible. In their daily travels, they were enjoying the fruits of a policy decision made five decades earlier, with the City of Delft's 1970 Vervoersen Verkeersplan (Transport and Traffic Plan).

Authored by Delft University of Technology (then Technische Hogeschool Delft) professor Jacques Volmuller, in response to a mounting safety crisis caused by the growing volumes and speeds of cars on urban streets, this traffic circulation plan began with the fundamental idea that every child should be able to walk safely to school, a shop, or a friend's house without crossing a busy (and dangerous) arterial road.

Like many other global cities in the 1960s, Delft came under immense pressure from engineers and economists to quickly "modernize" itself, with proposals to build intensive road networks with broad thoroughfares, expansive intersections, oversized bridges, and acres of parking. This required the demolition of large parts of the inner city and its surrounding neighborhoods, some of which actually began to take place in the Oude Stad (Old City), before protests by local students and residents successfully urged the City to take a different approach.

The spatial demands of a car-centric city were glaringly irreconcilable with Delft's small, compact nature, so Volmuller's top-down, wholistic plan was embraced as a substitute. Critically, it dealt with the management of car traffic, public transport, and cycling as separate—but interconnected—mobility networks.

Recognizing that the most effective way to control a hazard is to physically eliminate it, this policy—and subsequent circulation plans implemented on a neighborhood-by-neighborhood basis—purposely prevented drivers from cutting through living areas by pushing them to an outer ring road the moment they left their front door. Not only did removing these *sluiproutes* (sneaky routes) create streets more welcoming for people of all ages to walk and cycle, but it also made those more desirable modes more direct and convenient. This was accomplished through the concept of "filtered permeability," which prevented through traffic on most streets, while people on foot and bike were permitted to trickle through (and even travel the wrong way on one-way streets). As Dutch planners have discovered over the years, the most important part of an effective walking and cycling plan is the car plan. But this car management plan must be implemented in parallel with a viable alternative to driving short distances—in this case a dense, well-connected cycling network.

We felt these invisible forces within a week of arriving, having overestimated the size of Etienne's bedroom and finding ourselves faced with the task of taking the bed we had ordered back to IKEA. Located just outside the ring road on Delft's east side, on the A13 motorway, the warehouse was a 2.9-kilometer (1.8-mile) "straight shot" on foot, bike, or bus from our westside apartment. When we loaded the flatpack into our rental car and punched in the GPS coordinates, we were looking at a circuitous, 10.5-kilometer (6.5-mile) journey around the perimeter of the city.

By making a clear distinction between circulating traffic, through traffic, and destination traffic, the policy served as a precursor to the classifications adopted in the Netherlands in 1992 with Duurzaam Veilig (Sustainable Safety). It dictated that all roads should fall into one of three categories:

1. Stroomwegen (Flow Roads)—motorways limited to 100 km/h or 60 mph

2. Gebiedsontsluitingswegen (Distributor Roads)—arterials limited to 50 km/h or 30 mph within built-up areas
3. Erftoegangswegen (Access Roads)—30 km/h or 20 mph residential streets

This system did not recognize roads with the dual functions of through traffic and destination traffic, such as arterial roads that doubled as busy retail corridors. This can generally be seen as a positive move, but it failed to acknowledge Delft's existing street pattern and structure, with a number of dense residential and commercial developments built hastily along key routes after the Second World War. To square that circle, the City of Delft retained its own fourth category of road, which it had called the Wijkontsluitingsweg (District Access Road).

In an attempt to satisfy their dual and conflicting purposes, District Access Roads are calmed to 40 km/h (25 mph) and incorporate important pedestrian safety elements and segregated cycle tracks, with careful attention to the design of side streets, crossings, and intersections. The desired speed is achieved not by passively posting a sign (the police can't be everywhere, and drivers will travel as fast as they feel comfortable), but by actively engineering means that force drivers to slow down and pay attention, such as brick medians, narrow lanes, and textured paving. Dutch police actually do very little traffic enforcement. If too many drivers speed on a street, it is deemed a design failure and sent back to the drawing board.

Another critical detail seen on these streets is the raised and continuous foot and cycle path. At each point where the parallel sidewalk and cycle track cross a side street, rather than disappear and drop into the driving zone (as is common in most cities), cars are ramped up a few centimeters into the walking and cycling area—and treated as a trespasser—before going back down again. By keeping the vulnerable road users in a prioritized, elevated, seamless space, drivers must reduce their speed and increase their vigilance, reducing any sense of entitlement.

Early versions of Wijkontsluitingswegen failed to include this detail, giving the impression that drivers had priority when entering side streets. Signage that implored them to yield was generally ignored, causing a number of collisions. In response, the raised and continuous path was introduced to physically manage the serious clash between cars turning to cross and pedestrians and cyclists traveling straight ahead in the walking and cycling area.

This hierarchy of streets is administered carefully to direct cars out of the local neighborhoods at slow speeds, onto arterial roads where they can accelerate slightly, and then onto regional motorways where they no longer impact urban life. The Distributor and District Access Roads form a loose grid with a mesh of about 1 kilometer (0.6 miles), but often deviate, directing cars away from sensitive areas, such as canals, rivers, churches, and plazas. This means that on the vast majority of Delft streets, the car traffic moves around the same speed as the bicycle traffic.

Significantly, within built-up areas, these arterial roads are rarely more than one lane of traffic in each direction (often with a row of street trees, a grass median, or a dedicated bus lane and tramway running down the middle). This means that, with a requisite midblock island, vulnerable pedestrians—especially children and the elderly—are seldom exposed to risk for more than 2.5 meters (8 feet) while crossing the street. Multilane roads may have served a purpose decades ago, when not every internal combustion engine was created equal, but Dutch engineers are gradually removing them from urban environments, since they encourage drivers to exceed the desired (and safe) speed. As they have discovered over years of such "road diets," a street's capacity is not determined by its width but by the design of its intersections. By getting the junction design right, usually with unsignalized treatments (like a roundabout), a single-lane road can handle as much traffic as a two-lane road, while maintaining flow and minimizing wait times for all users.

Sending car drivers on extended detours around the city seems frustrating and time intensive, but as transport planners stress, the opposite often turns out to be true. By moving traffic from slower access streets to faster distributor roads, and reducing congestion by offering viable alternatives for short-distance trips, driving times often end up being less than had drivers taken the direct route. Ultimately, the stated

Delft's Papsouwselaan is a Distributor Road. It is 50 meters (164 feet) wide and has one car lane in each direction, a dedicated bus lane/tramway, and two bidirectional cycle tracks. (Modacity)

goal is accomplished—children are allowed to wander freely and safely around their city, the textbook definition of a win–win scenario.

Restoring the Freedom to Roam

Within a short period of time, Etienne and Coralie have completely and successfully integrated into Dutch life. They navigate the city as well as—if not better than—their parents do. The very things we had hoped for them have become normal parts of their everyday life: getting out of the house regularly to meet with friends, enjoying a walk or bike ride through their neighborhood, or heading out for ice cream in the city center. As parents, we are far less worried about their safety, and we see their confidence so clearly written on their faces. Delft is now their home. They know the places they want to go and exactly how to get there, and they can do it all by themselves.

Of course, they will experience minor hiccups along the way, as Etienne did with his little spill. And yes, Coralie has still gotten lost on more than one occasion. But we are safe in the knowledge that we live in a city that provides countless opportunities for our children to assess and take calculated risks, and through that process, prove their resiliency on a near-daily basis. In such a place, a tumble off a bicycle into a grass median will likely end in a slight injury. But without that lenient infrastructure, such a small mistake could result in something much worse—if not deadly. Shouldn't all children get to grow up in such a forgiving environment?

In recent months, Coralie has gotten into the delightful habit of cooking dinner one night per week. Bringing home a recipe from her high school class, she cycles to the local Albert Heijn (a grocery store chain), purchases everything she needs, and prepares a delicious meal from scratch. Other nights, if Mom or Dad is cooking and is missing a key ingredient, Etienne can go to the store to pick it up. It is a reminder that such early independence—in both transport and day-to-day life—benefits the parents as much as it does the children. In a culture where the majority of supervision and housework still falls on the mother's shoulders, this presents a disproportionate advantage to the matriarch of the family.

One Sunday toward the end of July 2019, it suddenly came into focus exactly what these decades-old traffic policy decisions meant to our little family. Coralie had made plans to meet friends at a swimming pool in The Hague, while her brother cycled to the nearby Drievliet amusement park, leaving the pair of us (part-time) empty nesters to play tourists in our new hometown. We enjoyed a wonderful day hopping between the centuries-old historic sites of Delft, using our newly acquired Museumkaart—including the birthplace of Johannes Vermeer and the burial place of William van Oranje—while the kids entertained themselves many miles away.

In between stops, we toasted Belgian beers in the Beestenmarkt and reflected on how much our lives had changed in a few short months. In a different context, those journeys to the pool and theme park would demand four additional car trips by Mom or Dad. Extrapolate that daily travel to sport activities, music classes, and friends' houses across a typical week, and you suddenly realize how the backseat generation creates additional strain on our streets, our wallets, and our lives.

Coralie and a friend partaking in a regular custom for teenagers (and adults) in the Netherlands: *achterop zitten* (sitting on the back) on her Gazelle bicycle. (Modacity)

This is not to say that Dutch parents don't experience the stresses of childrearing and the commitments that go with it. But there is much to be said about the fact that in this environment, we no longer dedicate much of our time outside work—time that should be spent recharging for the next day—worried about which child has which activity when, and who is going to get them there. The additional mental and emotional energy we used to spend choreographing the lives of four people has certainly lessened with our children's newly discovered autonomy, and we are savoring those effects every day. The results are confident, more independent children and much more chilled out parents. Building autonomous cities doesn't just lead to happier kids, it leads to happier parents too!

Chapter 2

The Connected City

Neither television nor illegal drugs has been the chief destroyer
of American communities. Instead, the automobile has that
dubious honor.
— Jane Jacobs

ll it took was a split second. One momentary lapse in focus, and our relationship with our street and our neighbors would forever change. After seeing Chris and the kids off to work and school, respectively, and finishing her last few sips of coffee in peace, Melissa stepped out of the house, closing the front door behind her to start the day. In that instant she realized she had forgotten to remove the second key from the inside, a common feature of many double-sided Dutch locks. "Maybe it'll be okay," she thought to herself, scrambling to unlock the door, and hoping all would be well. It would not. As she feared, the other key blocked her from unlocking the door from the outside, leaving everyone locked out of the house.

We had been living in Delft for two months and settling into our routines. Relationships were starting to form with classmates and colleagues, but we had yet to really meet our neighbors. In Vancouver, we had had the good fortune of living in a thirty-unit cooperative housing complex, forcing us to get to know our neighbors from day one. But beyond the front gates of our building, that was far from the case. Our street was not a place where people gathered and hung out, and as a result, we rarely passed a familiar face.

In Delft, our previous lived experience combined with the obvious language barrier and our own bashfulness when it comes to introducing ourselves to new people, meant that we had managed just a few awkward waves to passing neighbors and brief chit-chat with the kind woman living next door. We had yet to make any meaningful connections with the people living around us. This isn't to say that social behavior wasn't happening around us; we frequently saw groups of neighbors sharing their day with each other. We just hadn't had the opportunity to participate—yet.

So, in that moment, realizing she was not getting back into the house without a great deal of effort, and feeling completely alone, Melissa panicked. A quick call to Chris revealed he was stuck in a meeting and unable to help. An attempt to reach through the mail slot and knock out the key with various items proved fruitless, and it became abundantly clear: she was not going to fix this mess on her own.

"Kun je me helpen?" Melissa put her first weeks of Dutch lessons to use, knocking on our next-door neighbor's door. Marieke—whom we had referred to as our "deck neighbor," because our terrace looks over to hers—listened intently to the problem, explained in broken English that she was about to head to work, but knew exactly who could help. They walked across the street and knocked on another door. A red-haired gentleman answered wearing a giant, welcoming smile on his face. "This is Peter and he is always good at finding solutions," Marieke declared.

"Yes! Of course! Come in and we will figure this out," proclaimed Peter enthusiastically. While Melissa wasn't exactly sure what she expected would happen, what followed is a series of events that cemented our social connection to our neighbors and our street.

"Let's see what we can do!" Peter announced. "But first . . . coffee!" We have come to learn that very few things in this country are more sacred than the coffee break. So Peter and Melissa shared a coffee in his living room while discussing our family's move to the Netherlands: the positives, the negatives—besides our current predicament—and how our Dutch was coming along. "We leren, maar niet snel," she responded with her limited vocabulary, letting him know that we were learning, but only slowly. Peter then revealed he had lived on this street

A standard residential street in Delft, which specifically reduces motor vehicle speed through design: width-narrowing chicanes (staggered buildouts), speed humps, and texture. (Modacity)

his entire life, and his three brothers still reside here. In fact, the gentleman living directly across from us (and next door to Peter) was his brother Chris, who walked in, trailed by Tiger, his cat. This was becoming a family affair!

Over coffee, Melissa also learned that Peter is the volunteer *klusjesman* (handyman) at Etienne's school, and he had recognized Etienne while he was unlocking his bike on the sidewalk. "I will be sure to say 'hi' to him next time I see him!" he said warmly. As the coffee break came to a close, Peter proceeded to locate a locksmith, speaking in Dutch and relieving Melissa of the task of stumbling through her broken version, an experience she was not ready to relive following Etienne's hospital visit. He generously called several places and decided on one that was the closest and most affordable (ah, that famous Dutch frugality!). Told it would be an hour until the locksmith arrived, they savored another cup of coffee, joined by three other fellow neighbors, while they waited for the locksmith.

When Melissa finally made it to the office that morning, and a few of her colleagues had a chuckle over her rookie mistake, she recounted how one misstep had led to meeting several neighbors—a genuine silver lining. In the space of a few hours, we had come to appreciate how our traffic-calmed street had created the ideal conditions for an introduction to the people who live along it, as well as their own social circle, providing more than the occasional "good morning."

Despite a certain familiarity with our fellow housing cooperative neighbors in Vancouver, we came to Europe with a pessimistic view of finding friends on our street. Our social networks would likely come from work, some connections we had made online, and the odd parent of our children's friends. Instead, we had quickly built meaningful contacts with a number of our "streetmates," leading to our suddenly feeling a strong sense of belonging to our new community.

There is an amazing comfort in knowing that the people living around you care enough to look out for you. Even for us as strangers from another land, the fallout from that little mistake has led to "stop-and-chats" in the city center, smiles as we cross paths on the cycle tracks, and waves through our front window as our neighbors pass by. Peter did—and continues to—say "hello" to Etienne at school, and Marieke often speaks Dutch to the children, while their parents offer the occasional "Goedemiddag" (good afternoon). We've even been convinced to leave a key with one of them, "just in case" (as it turns out, this would not be the last time we managed to lock ourselves out). Over the months, we've met a few others on our street, as it is customary to accept packages for neighbors if they're not home to accept them; leading us to gifting a bottle of wine to the couple two doors down for receiving a plethora of Christmas parcels from Canada throughout December.

Of course, this is not solely a Dutch phenomenon, and these are all the smallest of gestures, which in many contexts, wouldn't seem that noteworthy. But for these Canadians, the chain of events that stemmed from the moment the front door locked behind Melissa proved to be the building blocks for a sense of community we could never have anticipated. We no longer feel isolated or alone on the street where we live. We're a genuine part of the neighborhood. Those bonds are so strong, in fact, that we now feel remiss in our neighborliness when we think of eventually leaving our rental flat to buy a home elsewhere.

What makes this particular street so different from the ones we had previously lived on in Vancouver (and other Canadian cities) is complex. It has as much to do with the human response to social interactions as it does the built environment in which they take place. The connection we now have with our neighborhood—and the feelings it instills in us go beyond the comfort of simply knowing our neighbors—will have a lasting effect on us for years to come. Because, as we would learn and experience for ourselves, the social cohesion of a city—and the mental and physical well-being of its residents—is shaped greatly by the design of its streets and neighborhoods.

Disconnected through Street Design

When it comes to the evolution of the modern cityscape, one thing is certain: the rise of automobility has inextricably changed the concept of a street from a place to stay in to a place to pass through. The sociability of those streets has been dramatically reduced as the volume and speed of motor vehicles increases. This is evidenced in the switch of the street from being a *child space* to an *adult space*, but also in the lack of familiarity with neighbors experienced by swathes of individuals the world over. In 1974, nearly a third of Americans reported spending time with their neighbors at least twice a week. Forty years later, that number had been cut in half. Over the same period of time, the number of Americans reporting zero interactions with their neighbors has grown from 20 percent to almost 35 percent.

The definitive account of this phenomenon is found in a 2020 update to the 1981 book *Livable Streets* by urban designer and theorist Donald Appleyard. In the chapter "Streets Can Kill Cities: Third World Beware," he coins the term *auto-mania* (or *auto-mobility industrial complex*) to warn the developing world of what he saw in US cities, whose streets were dead from a social viewpoint: "The automobile, satisfier of private needs, demands, and whims, has created an insatiable demand for access, and a whole profession of planners and engineers both serving and further stimulating that demand. The result has been cities with streets and street systems dedicated to the automobile to the virtual exclusion of all other uses."

Tragically, Appleyard was killed by a drunk driver in Athens just one year after his book was published, but since then, his son Dr. Bruce Appleyard, an associate professor at San Diego State University, has built on his father's legacy. In 2020, he published *Livable Streets 2.0*, a further examination of the conflict, power, and promise of our streets. It includes a seminal 1971 study of three corridors in San Francisco, each similar in size and context but with varying volumes of traffic, exploring the impacts these levels have on the street's sociability and livability.

Appleyard Sr. began this research shortly after Bruce was hit by a car at the age of 4. As Bruce recounts, the focus of both the original and the revised texts is the dependency our society has on cars, and what that means for the characteristics of streets. "We build roads to satisfy the needs of traffic," he says, "but the effect of that traffic is a hidden harm; it's harder to see." Because the focus of engineers is primarily on *level of service*—the mechanism used to determine how well a facility is operating from a driver's perspective—there is little-to-no attention given to what it feels like to actually "exist" in that space outside of an automobile.

The streets chosen for the study fell into three distinct categories: light (2,000 vehicles per day at 30 km/h or 20 mph), moderate (8,000 vehicles per day at 40 km/h or 25 mph), and heavy (16,000 vehicles per day at 60 km/h or 35 mph). Those classification names were important: in the transportation field, traffic is usually measured in terms of low, medium, or high volumes. By using a more "weighted" terminology, Dr. Appleyard believed his father wanted to demonstrate the gravity of the impacts. Residents were then asked to respond to specific questions focused on variables such as comfort, safety, noise, social interaction, and the overall identity of the street. Since they were published nearly 50 years ago, the results have proved incredibly convincing in demonstrating the destructive power of traffic on residents' connection to their streets and their community.

One of the most striking observations was how heavier volumes of traffic pushed activity that would normally happen in the front of the home toward the rear. "Where light traffic knits a community together, heavy traffic rips it apart," Dr. Appleyard says. Residents along the heavy traffic street reported having three times fewer local friends (just 0.9 per respondent) and two times fewer acquaintances than those on the light traffic street. They were also less likely to visit neighbors, and identified a smaller area as their "personal territory." This had a distinct effect on the perceptions of their street, and whether they considered it to be "friendly." With a lower feeling of kinship to their street and their neighbors, those living on the heavy street lacked the social interactions that made them feel a part of their community. Instead, neighbors didn't appear to look out for each other, and the public realm was thought of solely as a hostile space dedicated to the movement of strangers.

Dr. Appleyard refers to this situation as a *street in conflict*. Where a *street at peace* encourages interactivity—talking to neighbors, children playing, and similar activities—a street in conflict is one where the car travels through and pushes people away, causing their ultimate withdrawal from the street itself. At its core, enabling the conflict between cars and residents restricts and even eliminates interaction on the street. "Studies have focused almost exclusively on increasing traffic capacity through devices such as street widening, signalization, and one-way streets with no parallel accounting of the environmental and social costs of these alterations," he declares.

At the same time, due to the unfriendliness of the street, residents were not only less acquainted with their neighbors, but the continuous presence of strangers, even in passing cars, evoked feelings of fear and distrust. The proverbial "stop-and-chat" was not common practice, leading to even greater retreat from the community.

Much like Dr. Karsten's idea of the city as an archipelago, these heavy traffic streets create a *barrier effect* (also called *community severance*). According to Dr. Appleyard's research, this refers to "how wider roads and increased motor vehicle traffic volumes and speeds cause delay, discomfort and reduced access to active modes (walking, bicycling and their variants), as well as a resident's ability to build social cohesion

HEAVY TRAFFIC

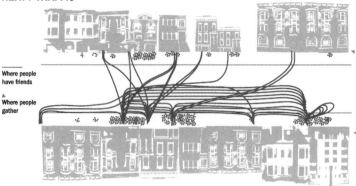

Where people
have friends

Where people
gather

MODERATE TRAFFIC

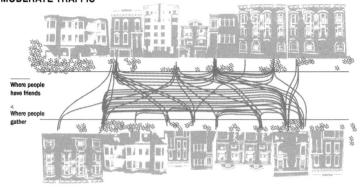

Where people
have friends

Where people
gather

LIGHT TRAFFIC

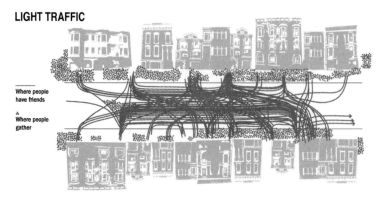

Where people
have friends

Where people
gather

"Where light traffic knits a community together, heavy traffic rips it apart."
The dramatic impact that vehicle volumes have on the social life of a street.
(Bruce Appleyard)

(positive relationships among neighbors)." Therefore, he has taken his father's work one step further to focus on how traffic calming can be the glue that holds the care of the street and its residents together. "Streets should be a place where we share our humanity. Streets are for our humanity," he reminds us. Looking more closely at Dr. Appleyard's research, it becomes clear that the incompatibility between drivers and residents has a sustained impact on the streets they are expected to share. "It cognitively limits the sense of the home territory," he explains. "The barrier effect limits people's cognitive sense of ownership and place."

Think about it in its simplest terms: a lack of sense of ownership in the space outside your front door leads to taking care of what matters most: the space inside your own home. In Appleyard Sr.'s original research, residents' sense of personal territory seldom extended to the busy street, and for residents in apartments, that was often restricted to the space within their unit. "The gauge becomes, how far are you willing to rake the leaves beyond your own front steps?" Dr. Appleyard asks. If the street itself doesn't encourage people to be outgoing and connect to their community, they are reluctant to accept any responsibility for it and its care.

This insular and selfish thinking is a direct result of the livability—or lack thereof—of a street, especially one with heavy traffic volumes. Residents have little sense of joy and contentment in the space outside where they live. The front of the house is seen as where they leave the comfort of their home and enter the hostility of the world around them. Why bother taking care of it if they don't spend time there? As it turns out, aside from having feelings of belonging and pride for our immediate surroundings, the resulting lack of socialization has even greater impacts on the emotional and physical health of residents. That hidden harm Dr. Appleyard refers to extends far beyond the comfort of the street to our individual welfare.

Why Face-to-Face Contact Matters

As transportation networks have effectively engineered physical and social activity out of our lives, many people have lost the ability to

According to Dr. Appleyard, a street in conflict is one where the car travels through and pushes people away, and they ultimately withdraw from the street itself. (Modacity)

spontaneously meet their neighbors or make random connections with members of their community in public places. In her book *The Village Effect*, Canadian author and developmental psychologist Susan Pinker explores the importance of these moments of face-to-face contact. "When the car became the dominant form of transportation, the post office, newsstand, bookstore, and videostore—all places where we crossed paths just a few years ago—became obsolete," she writes on page 13. Decades later, the result is a level of loneliness that could be said, without hyperbole, to be reaching epidemic levels; a trend only compounded by lockdown conditions during the COVID-19 pandemic.

Forging close personal relationships is vital to humanity in many ways. It is how we learn compassion, empathy, and cooperation from an early age, and how we continue to learn and grow throughout our lives. Just having someone with whom to celebrate triumphs and talk

Through her research, Pinker found regular interaction with close personal relationships increases one's life expectancy by an average of 15 years. So it should come as no surprise that lonely people are more likely to experience serious health issues and premature death than their socially connected counterparts. A 2020 report from the National Academies of Sciences found that isolation was associated with a significantly increased risk of premature mortality from all causes, including dementia, coronary heart disease, cancer, functional decline, and stroke.

But what about those who experience a sudden loss, such as a spouse or life partner? Unfortunately, when a lifelong bond severs, it can directly impact the survivor's mortality. It's called the *widowhood effect*, which refers to the frequent occurrence of widowed people dying soon after the death of a spouse. Generally speaking, women tend to fair better as widows, living longer than men, a result directly linked to their having a reliable community to call on for social support.

Strong, meaningful social connections are vital to a sense of fulfillment and assimilation in a community. They are also integral to our sustained physical and mental health, impacting even our mortality. So how can our cities better foster opportunities to forge those bonds? Is it possible to create streets that benefit everyone, and not just the people using them for transportation? The answer is yes, and the good news is that the ingredients needed to build such streets were discovered decades ago, in the same Hof van Delft neighborhood our family now calls home.

Streets That Foster Social Connection

As Donald Appleyard warned in 1981, in the growing conflict between those who create traffic and those living next to it, urban planners had inexplicably taken the side of the former, leading to all kinds of hidden (and not-so-hidden) consequences. In a short period of time, many other cities acquiesced and stood by while cars carved up the social fabric of their communities. More than 10 years earlier, barely 200 meters (650 feet) from the street where our family would settle, a grassroots movement rose up in rejection of those priorities, sparking a citywide experiment that would lead to the development of an entirely new type of residential street.

As the story goes, before Professor Volmuller's 1970 Traffic Circulation Plan could be fully implemented across Delft, residents of the 50-meter (165-foot) long Tuinstraat (Garden Street) were watching in horror as the space outside their front door became increasingly hostile to children, with drivers using it as a shortcut between two adjacent streets. So, feeling abandoned by City staff, they opted to take matters into their own hands; one morning they erected concrete barriers and planted trees at each entry, effectively squatting the area for playing and socializing. Despite initially fighting this act of civil disobedience, the municipality eventually conceded, anticipating a renewal of the public space and surrounding houses, thereby beginning a decade-long process of redefining and redesigning its streets.

Out of that process, undertaken in coordination with the nearby Technical University, arose the concept of the *woonerf* (living street), a made-in-Delft solution where vehicle speeds were curbed to 15 km/h (10 mph), and pedestrians were given the full width of the street (which typically lacked any raised curbs). Considered extensions of the living room, *woonerven* were envisaged as outdoor spaces for the play and socialization of residents—especially children—where cars were allowed to move and park, but only within strict limitations. *Woonerven* were thus avoided by most cars (except the occasional local). Inhabitants were then provided with a semiprivate space in front of their home, to personalize with planting and seating.

The *woonerf* was quickly embraced by the national government, which issued specific guidelines and traffic rules for their implementation. These were adopted by dozens of local authorities, including Amsterdam, The Hague, Eindhoven, Groningen, and Utrecht. They consisted of five key features: a clear and distinct entranceway, shared space between cars and pedestrians, physical traffic-calming measures, limited on-street parking, and the incorporation of landscaping and furnishings.

First and foremost, entering a *woonerf* involves a greeting from a formal, distinct entranceway, making it clear you need to adjust your behavior accordingly. This can be as simple as having to cross over

Delft's Tuinstraat, home of the very first *woonerf* (living street), initiated by residents who effectively squatted the area for playing and socializing. (Modacity)

a continuous footpath, or speed hump—providing the sense of leaving the car space—but it may also incorporate trees, planter boxes, light fixtures, curb extensions, and bike parking. Out-of-scale signage is generally discouraged, seen as clutter to the streetscape, and replaced with design elements which emphasize that the space is for people rather than traffic.

Where possible, the car and pedestrian space should be shared on the same plane, with no clearly defined curb or "travel lane." This ambiguity between walking, cycling, and driving is critical to slowing drivers (and cyclists) down, and giving people on foot, especially kids, free rein to move (and linger) in the street.

·Physical traffic calming measures are essential to the design of a *woonerf*, the most important of which are changes to the linearity of the street. The introduction of a winding pathway disrupts the driver's sightline, discouraging drivers from looking too far ahead and racing through. Other elements include reduced width, speed humps, raised intersections, chicanes (bulb-outs that force drivers to move in a more serpentine pattern), one-way features, and changes in paving texture. Dutch engineers have spent decades mastering ways to trick drivers into traveling at the desired speed, especially using the latter. Bricks are ubiquitous on residential streets, as they create a fair amount of noise and vibration inside a car, leading the driver to voluntarily slow down.

In order to avoid the endless rows of standing steel—or "car canyons"—that line most residential streets, on-street parking should be restricted. Rather, availability should be limited and available only to local residents. This helps to restore the sightlines and "openness" of the street, inspiring more free movement across the street for children to play and residents to gather. Limited parking also prevents cars from becoming the predominant element. On many *woonerven*, space for parking is provided intermittently, punctuated by street trees, planters, lamp posts, and bike racks.

Last but not least, outdoor furniture and landscaping should be used to make the street more attractive; reclaiming it as a space for spending time. This includes trees and shrubs, sitting areas, play equipment, and places for communal dining. Bike parking, like car parking, must be provided, because much of cycling's time advantage is lost if secure parking isn't available within a short distance.

In the years after those brave Tuinstraat residents rescued their street from passing cars, hundreds of *woonerven* spread to cities across the country. Their defiant act even inspired copycats across Europe, with similar treatments popping up in Hannover, Germany (*spielstraße* or play streets), Cardiff, Wales (home zones), and Basel, Switzerland (*begegnungszonen* or encounter zones).

These upgrades provided easily quantified benefits, such as reduced speeds and increased safety, as well as difficult-to-measure improvements to the sociability of the street. In Hannover, Brenda Eubank-Ahrens observed that "children (and indirectly, their parents) felt more secure, allowing for proliferation of types of play and contact with adults. . . . Verbal communication expanded, and involvement with the physical environment generally increased, making the street livelier." In Cardiff, Dr. Mike Biddulph found that "residents stayed in the home zone for longer periods, engaging in optional activities and also socializing." And in Basel, researcher Daniel Sauter concluded that residents "felt more at home, lived there for longer periods, found their streets to be distinctive, and that their streets provided everything that they needed for a happy life when compared to busier streets."

Despite these quantitative and qualitative successes, by 1983, it was determined that *woonerven* were simply too costly to build and maintain on a broad scale, especially with the relocation and maintenance of underground utilities. Five years later, the Dutch government rolled out a 30 km/h (20 mph) residential street design standard, which would form the basis for the "Access Road" in the 1992 Sustainable Safety policy. While not having quite the same intention and execution as the *woonerf*, it draws heavily from its elements and has since been applied to almost every residential street in the country, ensuring that the streets remain safe *and* social places.

One further legacy of the *woonerf* concept is the *geveltuin* (facade garden) policy now found in the by-laws of almost every Dutch municipality, including Delft. Provided they meet a set of requirements—chiefly around preserving the width of the footpath—residents are encouraged to remove a patch of paving stones in front of their home and replace it with a green space. These climbing plants, shrubs, and flowers are combined with seating, resulting in a more personal and personalized streetscape, where people might actually want to spend their time in the public eye.

Making Streets Cozy Again

Having received a great deal of press in recent years, the Dutch expression *gezellig* is used in a wide variety of contexts and is difficult to translate directly into English, but it can best be described as a shared state of coziness or togetherness. While typically reserved for indoor settings, such as gathering with friends in a café or family in your living room, it is a concept that—we would argue—can be extended out the front door and onto the street, simply because of the unique way the space is designed.

Despite having a 15-meter (50-foot) right-of-way, similar to the street our family called home in East Vancouver, our new confines in Hof van Delft allocated the space between the three- and four-story buildings far differently. In Canada, the wide, smooth street—continuously lined on both sides by parked cars—invited drivers to use it as a shortcut between arterial roads. If anyone dared to step off the narrow footpath, over the curb and into the street, they were greeted with a honking horn by a passing driver, the ultimate expression that the space belonged to the drivers.

While not specifically a *woonerf*, our street in Delft checks many of its boxes, creating a place that feels *gezellig*. Not only does the circulation plan severely restrict the amount of through traffic, those few cars using the street—the vast majority of which are our neighbors—are reduced to much slower speeds through the use of offset features, narrowing, speed humps, chicanes, and textures. Combine those features with generous footpaths, periodic seating, and plentiful street trees, and you can perhaps appreciate our fondness for our new street and its inhabitants.

This affinity crystalized one summer's evening, when—having just returned from a week-long trip on the Eurostar to see family in the UK—we ran into Peter on the street. He proudly informed us that, earlier that week, he noticed the number 8 on our front door was fading, so he freshened it up with some paint! We thanked him profusely, surprised and delighted by this simple, but thoughtful neighborly act. That selfless act made all the more sense a few days later, when we peeked out of our living room window and spotted Peter, Chris, and Marieke huddled across the street with a crew of construction workers. After two months of sewage pipe replacement that saw our entire street—every brick, paver, and curbstone—disassembled, loaded onto pallets, and trucked off; it was gradually being returned and reassembled, piece by painstaking piece. Our new friends were helping the men tasked with putting the footpath back together, carefully selecting the right stone for the job, and switching out pieces that didn't quite meet their satisfaction. Their feelings of pride and comradery transcended any sense of decorum. This was their street—the one Peter and Chris grew up on—and every brick had to be perfect.

It is obviously too simplistic to suggest that designing city streets in a more human way will single-handedly reverse the worsening

The *geveltuin* (facade garden) policy encourages residents to personalize the space outside their home with planting and seating. No special permit is required. (Modacity)

loneliness epidemic. But even as more and more people opt to live alone, as our three aging neighbors can attest, the impacts can be softened by creating communities that facilitate robust and relevant support systems. This can be accomplished by reversing the urban design paradigm, and once again prioritizing those who live next to traffic over those who create it.

Almost a year after our move to Delft, our family found itself spending a quiet New Year's Eve at home. After many months of change, stress, learning how to adapt to our new surroundings, and settling into our not-so-new-anymore lives, it was a welcome respite. As evening fell, we decided to take a walk through the city center to experience the Dutch phenomenon of setting off as many fireworks as possible to celebrate the dawning of a new year. As the only time of year it is legal to buy and use them, the city—and country—was in a constant state of eruption. And no, the irony of a nation that survived untold bombardments during the Second World War purposely setting off explosions for 24 consecutive hours was not lost on us.

Nevertheless, during that stroll, we saw many familiar faces gathering to take part in this tradition. Despite our Canadian disposition to think this all seemed rather dangerous—and it is, with far too many people ending up in the hospital each year—there was still something joyous about watching our community come together for a party. With quiet, cozy spaces, the streets were filled with revelers that hadn't traveled to the local bar to ring in the new year, as we were accustomed to do. Rather, they opted to celebrate among the people with whom they share a street.

Back in our apartment, we watched the television feed of festivities elsewhere as we counted down: "Drie! Twee! Één! Gelukkig Nieuwjaar!" followed by a rampage of explosions from every corner of the city, including our own street. Our neighbors had gathered to set off fireworks and wish each other the best for the coming year. We hesitantly joined them from our stoop and enjoyed the show, when suddenly they all raced over, one by one, to firmly shake our hands and tell us, "Beste wensen!" (Best wishes). It was our first holiday season away from Canada, and we would be lying if we said we weren't feeling a little homesick. This unexpected show of kindness and solidarity was such a heartwarming way to start our year that we overlooked our worry about the explosions and enjoyed the feeling of being a part of this welcoming community, brought together by little more than a postcode, and a street that made social connection the rule, rather than the exception.

Chapter 3

The Trusting City

Car drivers behave like a bunch of geese. They have the same distance from each other and fly at the same speed, and move almost in military formation. Cyclists move like a swarm of sparrows. There are thousands of them moving in chaos, but there are no collisions.
— Wim Bot

At first glance, the street crossing at Abtswoudseweg and Zuideinde appears no different from the countless other intersections that dot cities across the globe. As the merging point of two *fietsstraten* (bicycle streets, where cars are treated as guests), the adjoining Abtswoudsebrug serves as the main gateway to the TU Delft (Delft University of Technology) campus from Delft Station. But on closer inspection, despite being the busiest junction in the city—with 21,000 cyclists (one-fifth of the city's population!) passing through each weekday—it lacks the common features that would usually be expected to direct each user and control the flow of traffic. To the horror of foreign engineers who have spent their entire careers designing such intersections, this one successfully (and safely) functions without a single paint mark, road sign, or traffic light.

Within weeks of our arrival, Chris gleefully joined thousands of students, professors, and teaching assistants who pedal across the Delftse Schie River for their first class of the day, on his own way to the Dutch Cycling Embassy office at the southern edge of the university campus. Having reveled in the idea of pedaling shoulder-to-shoulder within the cycling masses, the first few instances were admittedly a little disarming. It wasn't long, however, before he learned that what appears from the outside to be a disorderly clutter is actually a carefully choreographed street ballet. Pedestrians, cyclists, and the periodic driver converge from every direction, exchanging subtle cues—eye contact, a hand signal, a warm smile, a bell ring, or even a brief word or two—with dozens of complete strangers, negotiating these complex situations and reaching a consensus, in one precise moment, who will yield to whom, and then moving onward with their day.

To a newcomer, the lack of formality and instruction at intersections like this across the Netherlands can be intimidating, especially when perched on the seat of a bicycle. We will never forget the sheer look of terror in Melissa's father's eyes when he negotiated that junction for the first time. In hindsight, although he was comfortable on a bike in his Canadian suburb, perhaps introducing a 62-year-old to Dutch cycling with a ride through TU Delft during orientation week wasn't the brightest idea.

There is little doubt that a human-powered, human-scale transport network *feels* more chaotic than one dominated by motor vehicles; the latter of which is, by its nature, orderly. But when three-quarters of trips are made on foot or bike—as they are in Delft—social trust and interaction are ideal ways to create free-flowing traffic situations, without the need for stop-start, car-based engineering.

For our family, there was undoubtedly an adjustment period, but before long, all four of us were fluent in the complex choreography that takes place every day on Delft's busy streets. After a month or two, we were comfortably navigating rush hour traffic on foot or bike, displaying the same calm confidence as everyone around us, and even starting to develop faith in their predictability. We found a common language learned and passed forward with every interaction at every intersection. It wasn't long, for example, before Coralie proudly shared a revelation she had made on her ride home from school one afternoon: when an approaching cyclist stops moving their feet, they are preparing to turn by applying their pedal-brake.

On the rare occasion that a situation was misjudged, leading to a close call or even a fender bender, it was the result of a minor breakdown in communication, or a flaunting of the unwritten code that

Over 21,000 cyclists pass through the crossing at Abtswoudseweg and Zuid-einde each day, without requiring a single paint mark, road sign, or traffic light. (Modacity)

exists. More often than not, when this occurs one easily adjusts their speed and/or direction, and offers an apologetic nod or hand wave to the affronted party. On their first few morning rides to school, Chris and Etienne witnessed two or three such incidents. The most notable part was that, unlike when two cars collide at high speeds, the conflict between two slow-rolling cyclists was a total "nonevent," with both parties dusting themselves off, politely acknowledging their mistake, and then pedaling off in separate directions.

Much of this unique social dynamic is supported by the "sit-up-and-beg" geometry of the ubiquitous Dutch bike, a style all four members of our family had been comfortably riding in Vancouver for many years, and of course continue to ride. These bikes allow for the maximum engagement of our senses; senses that are otherwise dulled when one is cocooned in the shell of a car. While most bike frames force riders to lean forward and strain their neck to make visual contact with others, the vertical posture of a Dutch bicycle affords our family a clear, unfil-tered view of surrounding people and places. The average speed of 10

Unlike the rider's posture on most "dropped" bike frames, one's vertical posture on a Dutch bicycle affords a clear, unfiltered view of surrounding people and places. (Modacity)

to 15 km/h (6 to 10 mph) is optimal for using one's entire body to send and receive nuanced signals with pedestrians and cyclists—a sideways glance, a pointed finger, or the drop of a shoulder—sometimes several meters before arriving at a given intersection. Even the standard back-pedal brakes, as our daughter had astutely observed, provide more clues during a negotiation than brakes tucked under the handlebars.

Enabling people to move around their city in such a fluid and effortless manner has the added bonus of allowing them to cycle significant distances without needing to put their foot down. Anyone who has ridden a bike can attest to the importance of momentum, and there is something incredibly liberating about living in a place that actually prioritizes its continuous motion. For Chris's new daily 4-kilometer (2.5-mile) commute to the office, he pedals through 20 different (three- or four-legged) intersections, including the afore-mentioned Abtswoudsebrug. Just three of these junctions make use of traffic lights—not one has a stop sign—and in each case, pedestrians and cyclists have a continual green light, and drivers must "beg" for permission to cross the foot and cycle path by triggering a sensor in the ground. This extends to road works, where *fietsers afstappen* (cyclists dismount) signs are seldom seen, because they disadvantage the elderly, infirm, and people carrying kids and/or large items. In most cases, the priority is to keep the bicycles moving.

In contrast, Chris's former 5-kilometer (3-mile) commute from East Vancouver to his office in Fairview Slopes included 36 intersections, 16 of which were controlled with a stop sign or traffic light. In the case of the latter, each was programmed to prioritize the flow of crossing car traffic until people on foot or bike pressed a "beg button," leading to lengthy wait times. These delays would add anywhere from 10 to 15 minutes to what should have been a 20-minute journey.

With each passing day and passing ride, we gradually realized our preferred mode of transport exposes us to people and places we wouldn't otherwise see. This became particularly noticeable when we cycled to school with Etienne, who—because he was learning the Dutch language from "scratch"—has ended up traveling to the south-western neighborhood of Voorhof. With a high concentration of social and rental housing, it is one of the most diverse and densely populated parts of the country, with a large number of students, immigrants, and refugees. Sharing its cycle paths with the proverbial "other"—including men, women, and children of Turkish, Moroccan, and Ethiopian descent—allowed us to get out of our social and spatial bubble and provided us with a regular reminder of our common humanity.

After a full year of sharing these exchanges with fellow commuters on the streets of Delft, we have started to wonder how these casual interactions might impact the community as a whole. The Dutch are, after all, a very trusting society, as we had been told, and had even experienced firsthand on more than one occasion. We couldn't help but think that this was—at least in part—because of the way so many of them traveled around their cities, in constant communication with each other, building common empathy, acceptance, and understanding at an enormous scale. In an era where selfishness, skepticism, and tribalism reign supreme, how might those destructive tendencies be aggravated by experiencing much of the world through the windshield of an automobile?

The Windshield Worldview

Mobility, of course, is more than just "time spent" getting from A to B, and analyzing its sensory, emotional, and social qualities has been the lifelong pursuit of Dr. Marco te Brömmelstroet, professor of urban mobility futures at the University of Amsterdam. He points to a regrettable turning point, about a century ago, when transportation was captured mainly as a field for engineers and economists; professions that largely focus on the quantitative over the qualitative. They subscribed to the homo economicus (economic man) theory, which assumes all contributing members of society make consistently rational, narrowly self-interested choices, to maximize their utility as a consumer and profit as a producer.

Through that narrow lens, transportation was thought of as a simplistic system of "pipes" that had one purpose: to function effectively (i.e., not clog up). Since travel time was precious minutes and hours not spent maximizing economic output, it was seen as a wasteful disutility, something that should be minimized at all costs. Speed was to be increased and friction at street level decreased, and every other human being—whether on foot, on a bicycle, or in a car—became a competitor; an obstacle to the pace and progress of homo economicus. Congestion became a problem that must be solved, with little regard to cost or consequence, despite affecting only a relatively small percentage of the population. Little-to-no consideration was given to how this "wasted time" might impact human health, happiness, or social cohesion.

"The way in which we travel influences how we behave and ultimately who we are," explains Te Brömmelstroet, who, without putting too fine a point on it, maintains that the solitary space of the automobile reinforces feelings of selfishness, distrust, and a lack of cooperation with others. "You are alone in your car, convinced of the logic that you have the right-of-way, because you want to minimize your disutility," he suggests. Traveling at high speeds and cocooned by steel means all of your interactions at intersections are depersonalized. They are no longer negotiations between fellow human beings, but governed by technology—a *verkeersregelinstallatie* (traffic management installation)—that interferes from above; a computer program that decides and dictates who has the right-of-way.

Often one of the first collective qualities to erode when the private automobile becomes the predominant norm and mode of transportation is the level of *social trust*. Defined as the degree to which we believe the people around us can be trusted, it influences attitudes and behavior at all levels of society, where low measures of social trust mean a lack of confidence in our fellow neighbors, business colleagues, and public institutions. These values can influence national economic growth just as powerfully as financial and physical capital, and are associated with many other noneconomic outcomes, including quality of life and mental health.

The *World Values Survey*, which has tracked the degrees of social trust since the early 1980s, has shown the rates in America and Great Britain declining steadily, now at 35 and 30 percent, respectively. The Netherlands, meanwhile, has been trending in the opposite direction and is second only to Norway, with a level of 70 percent. While far from offering an overarching account, this starts to explain the rise of populism in the United States and United Kingdom (and its failure to largely gain traction in the Netherlands), caused by a general and growing lack of trust in government officials, media organizations, scientific experts, and fellow citizens.

Then there is the psychological effect of spending so much time looking at the rear ends of other cars, an act associated with subordination, where communication is a one-way street. "That's very inhumane," Te Brömmelstroet asserts. "It relates to feelings of narcissism and feelings of being ignored, because no one is looking at you." Simply put, it's like trying to speak to someone's back rather than their face, revealing why we sometimes resort to obscene names and gestures. When we spend two or three hours a day under such impersonal conditions, looking at others who can't see us, it deeply affects our psyche and how we might act.

How we get around doesn't just influence our behavior. Amazingly, it can also change the chemical makeup of our brains. As social primates, we have evolved to send and receive a great deal of information through eye contact and body language, most of which is lost behind the wheel of an automobile. Eye contact, for example, loses its efficacy at speeds of 30 km/h (20 mph). This inability to communicate at high speeds and distances, compounded by feelings of confinement, often manifests itself in the form of "road rage" when another driver seemingly acts out of turn.

More than just a blast of the horn and a few four-letter words, this response triggers the "fight or flight" portion of the brain, activating a cascade of hormones to be released within our central nervous system. Given enough of these incidents over a long enough period of time, our brain chemistry can be permanently altered, and we can become more angry, more antisocial, more distrustful, less likely to handle complex reasoning, and less likely to consider the consequences of our actions.

The simple act of moving around outside of a car could have the inverse effect. Already mentioned in the context of loneliness, sometimes known as the "cuddle hormone," oxytocin is secreted by the posterior lobe of the pituitary gland under specific circumstances, including breastfeeding, orgasm, and eye contact. It is also released when exercising our bodies outdoors, something as simple as a brisk walk or a bicycle ride, especially when we do it alongside other people. In addition to its physical benefits, like reducing blood pressure, oxytocin has been shown to improve trust, generosity, empathy, mutual reciprocity, and positive social behavior.

Of course, there is the undeniable feeling of potency that comes with wielding a machine that possesses so much kinetic energy—a feeling fed by decades of enabling marketing messages from the car industry. This leads to a significant power imbalance, as people outside of the vehicle experience feelings of inequity, fear, and anxiety solely by its mere presence. Te Brömmelstroet references the work of Austrian philosopher Ivan Illich, who wrote at length about how this particular mode of transport—which takes up vast amounts of space (and energy) to operate and store—works well for the elite, those who choose to travel long distances between geographically distant places. "But at the same time this limits the mobility and the right to the street for

We have evolved to send and receive a great deal of information through eye contact and body language, most of which is lost behind the wheel of a car. (Modacity)

all others," prompts Te Brömmelstroet. Sociologist Zygmunt Bauman goes even further in his criticism, saying, "Automobility fosters individuality, competition, rejection of collective responsibility, aggressiveness, and domination by way of movement, speed, and escape."

Despite coauthoring countless academic papers and an entire book on the subject, *Het Recht van de Snelste* (The right of the fastest), Te Brömmelstroet is cautious to make this discussion solely about cars versus bikes. As someone who is regularly found hunched over a carbon fiber racing bike, and catches himself falling into similar patterns of behavior as he exceeds 30 km/r (20 mph), it is more a question of speed than mode. He sees the development and marketing of faster, smarter, more powerful motorized bikes as an extension of the same troublesome thinking. "The car is not the problem, but it's the best symbol of the underlying problems," he insists. "The bicycle is not the solution, but the best symbol of the types of solutions that we're looking for." So how might these solutions be implemented to improve trust and empathy on the streets of our cities?

The Prisoner's Dilemma

To further understand why nonmotorized transport fosters unselfish behavior, Dr. Te Brömmelstroet brings up the prisoner's dilemma, a game theory about recurring negotiation. It imagines a hypothetical situation where two convicts are given the option either to betray each other by testifying or to cooperate with each other by remaining silent. It postulates that two people acting in their own self-interest will produce the worst possible outcome. In the context of the city, each time two road users approach each other, they are faced with the choice to compete or cooperate. According to the prisoner's dilemma, the latter will lead to the best imaginable result.

When we repeat this exercise enough times, with enough different people, we collect a learned set of behaviors—or heuristics—because we begin to learn how others are thinking and acting. If we are too aggressive, or not aggressive enough, this dynamic fails to work. "This develops a certain level of trust and altruism," claims Te Brömmelstroet, "where in certain situations you are willing to give up your personal utility, because you know if you do that it will lead to a higher optimal outcome." At a higher level, this theory suggests that all people are intrinsically good but must be provided with the right conditions to express that benevolent nature. Instead of acting in our narrow self-interest like homo economicus, we act with society's greater good in mind like homo ethicus (ethical human).

This series of transactions does more than just encourage cooperation. In many cases, it can increase exposure to diversity—something lost in the solitude of the daily house/car/office routine—leading to lower levels of prejudice. "If you meet people different from you, not only meet them but actively negotiate with them, that's not only optimal, but it's where you develop all kinds of other important characteristics. The main one is trust," reveals Te Brömmelstroet. Most streets and junctions in the Netherlands wouldn't function without this inherent trust.

Many, including Virginia Woolf in 1935, liken the movement of pedestrians and cyclists at a Dutch intersection to a murmuration of starlings, where hundreds, if not thousands of birds fly in undulating, carefully coordinated arrangements across the sky. Like those people, the birds have developed a basic set of heuristics, or emergent behavior that allows them to act as a unit without running into each other. By monitoring the location and speed of its six closest neighbors, each .bird adjusts its flight pattern to ensure separation (turning to avoid crowding its flock mates), alignment (turning toward the average heading of its flock mates), and cohesion (turning to move toward the average position of its flock mates). For this to work, it must trust its peers to behave in a consistent and predictable manner. This leads to one more reason why social trust can start dropping as driving becomes more prevalent on your streets. "If you are in a car, with this traffic light issue, you're never in a prisoner's dilemma, because this situation is solved by an external algorithm," reveals Te Brömmelstroet. And that state of affairs will only be worsened by the (seemingly inevitable) introduction of autonomous cars: "Imagine all of us being in self-driving vehicles. The algorithm of the self-driving car solves all of these conflicts by itself. Imagine doing that for a year, and what that would do to your sense of trust of others." On a smaller scale, this is already happening with ride-hailing services, such as Uber and Lyft, gradually diminishing our capacity to trust, and willingness to go out of our way to help one another. In both cases, we're outsourcing these street-level negotiations to an external third party, with little regard of the consequences.

One has only to delve into the comment section of an online article to appreciate how important that exposure to social and spatial diversity is in the twenty-first-century city. Accelerated by our digital interactions, we seem to be increasingly organizing ourselves back into tribes, showing solidarity with others like ourselves and aggression to those who differ. It is not just our communities that are becoming more segregated, we are starting to sort ourselves by political affiliation, educational level, and even transportation mode; something that serves as a destructive mental barrier on and off the streets. This tribalism is fed and aggravated by the misguided belief that we know what others are like, without actually knowing them. Lacking any direct experience of the "other," we develop all kinds of fearful fantasies that cause us anxiety and distress, fantasies that are effectively weakened through firsthand experience and cooperation. Far from that simplified view of time "wasted" getting from A to B, our modes of transport can go a long way toward creating these opportunities for collaboration, breaking down tribalism one interaction at a time.

Much has been written about the egalitarian nature of Dutch society, perhaps best epitomized by the saying "Niet gelijk, maar wel gelijkwaardig" (We're not the same, but we're worth the same). It is something that transcends their culture onto their streets. This is, after all, a nation where the prime minister and royal family regularly cycle. Regardless of age, income, ethnicity, or physical ability, everyone is afforded the same respect, dignity, and safety. That level playing field is chiefly a result of keeping the car under control and providing everyone an opportunity to use the street. Pedestrians and cyclists aren't the proverbial "other." They are your next-door neighbor, hairdresser, and city councilor. As it turns out, empathy is quite a powerful emotion when it comes to encouraging positive road safety behavior.

Being encouraged to cooperate through our modal choice isn't just limited to the street. It even stretches to the world of competitive sports. Consider, for example, the difference in dynamics between cycling and motor racing. "You can't win the Tour de France by riding by yourself in front of the group," points out Te Brömmelstroet. "The pack is so much stronger than the individual." Even in a major cycling race, there is an element of cooperation, not unlike a flock of starlings, where the leader of the pack still has to cooperate until a kilometer before the finish line. "There's this interesting element that you don't see in Formula One, for instance, where being in a group of cars destroys your individual aerodynamics," he explains.

It is difficult to pinpoint the myriad ways that Dutch street culture influences social and political culture, but for Te Brömmelstroet, those effects are strong and varied. "One of my theories is that we utilize this polder model, this culture of decision-making and cooperation, partly because we also do it on the roads," he theorizes. "We are raised to find a consensus." So how do cities outside the Netherlands design their streets and intersections to enjoy those similar benefits?

The Intersection of Social Trust

In the early 1990s, the Netherlands' Sustainable Safety program created a road hierarchy that encouraged calmer streets, enabling even their youngest citizens the freedom and right to travel safely and comfortably from A to B. At the intersection of these streets, their high degree of social trust is seen on a daily basis. From the moment they are first able to walk their streets to their final days, Dutch citizens are constantly and purposely placed in a situation where they have to acknowledge the people around them. This, in part, has created a mobility system that thrives in an environment of trust, and breaks down when that trust is lost.

With over 80 percent of streets in the country designated "access roads" and slowed to speeds of 30 km/h (20 mph) or less, social trust is a key ingredient in moving securely and seamlessly through the places these roads intersect. This is a result of deliberate ambiguity; rather than rely on traffic signals and signage to determine right-of-way, their absence forces each person to slow down, assess their surroundings, and act accordingly. In fact, Dutch engineers consider the existence of a stop sign a design failure. With the right traffic-calming measures, such as raised intersections, continuous footpaths, and lane narrowing, moving within these spaces increases vigilance and awareness, making a stop sign entirely redundant.

The heightened degree of social trust needed to navigate these streets may not have been the initial intention of the Sustainable Safety program, but it is definitely a welcome by-product. This specifically relates to two key principles of the policy, forgiveness and predictability. Forgiveness consists of designing road networks that recognize the fallibility of the roads' users, creating an environment where, in the case of human error, the risk of serious injury is reduced. Predictability employs street design that encourages foreseeable behavior so one can anticipate the movements of fellow road users, ultimately reducing the potential for conflict. These two concepts are applied to all elements of the Dutch road network, including intersections, resulting in a mobility system that necessitates collaboration over competition, and selflessness over selfishness.

This attitude toward unnecessary stop signs also holds true for traffic lights. As Melissa's colleague at Mobycon, Lennart Nout, continually emphasizes when presenting on intersection design, traffic lights are solely a *management* tool, and *not* a safety tool. In the context of Delft, planners implement lights only where 50 km/hr (30 mph) distributor roads intersect, as a means to manage traffic flows. The safety of users is never the primary goal, opting instead to use principles like protected intersections and road markings over technology whenever possible.

Perhaps the best example of this in Delft is one of the three points on Chris's commute where he might be forced to stop at a traffic light. After crossing the aforementioned Abtswoudsebrug and entering the TU Delft campus, the continuous cycle path intersects with Rotterdamseweg, a distributor road that transitions into a rather innocuous residential street as it crosses the cycle path. However, because of the sheer volume of cyclists entering and exiting the campus (remember, 21,000 cross the bridge on an average weekday), the sporadic driver could be forced to wait up to 15 minutes during peak hours for a break in the endless stream of cyclists (who are always prioritized in built-up areas). The lights at this intersection serve one purpose: to temporarily stem the tide of bicycles and allow a handful of drivers through, but only when triggered by the presence of a car. Not for safety, but for flow.

That's not to say that Delft is totally void of traffic lights. As mentioned earlier, where there is a crossing of distributor roads, the volume and speed of the cars traveling along them make signalized intersections necessary. When that traffic management is no longer required, however, such as outside of peak hours and on weekends, many of these lights change from phased or sensor-triggered signals to a yield signal, represented by a flashing orange light. In these instances, the intersections are treated in the same way as neighborhood access road junctions, where users reduce their speed, make eye contact, interact, and yield when needed.

To those accustomed to an environment that depends heavily on signals to appoint priority, this indistinct approach can understandably seem counterintuitive, and even dangerous. But consider what happens at a traditional North American intersection when there is a power outage: the lights automatically switch to a flashing red, and drivers are forced to slow down, take stock of the situation, give priority to vulnerable road users before yielding to the right, and then advancing only when the way is clear. This is no different from the Dutch approach to intersections; in both cases, when someone behaves in their own self-interest, they put themselves ahead of everyone else, and this competitive system breaks down. Collaborative behavior—built on trusting others in that shared space to act predictably and in accordance with their surroundings—ensures that everyone can move through the area with minimal stress, whether by foot, bicycle, or car.

Of course, most Distributor Road junctions across the Netherlands have one important distinction that further enables the safe and comfortable movement of all modes: protection. The protected intersection is a staple throughout the country and has been slowly permeating countless other global cities, including our former home of Vancouver. While there are many iterations, it is hard to argue that the Dutch principles should not be the global standard. What makes them so successful? Once again, it comes down to trust, or rather forced trust through intentional design.

The design elements of a protected intersection force visual contact between users and require a collaborative approach for each user to succeed. For drivers, a 12-meter (40-foot) turning radius combined with a minimum 5-meter by 5-meter (16-foot by 16-foot) curbside island means, when turning right, they approach the cycle path at a nearly 90-degree angle, bringing cyclists into clear view and reducing the chance of collision. Road markings, such as "shark's teeth" (triangles that point to the party that must yield) indicate who has priority, making behavior in the space unsurprising. In most cases, the approach lane is reduced to a single lane, eliminating the danger of cyclists not being seen by left-turning vehicles while right-turning vehicles wait.

Pedestrians fare even better in this design, which is logical given that they are the most at risk. First, the foot path is always placed behind the cycle path, meaning that turning vehicles must first cross the space for cycling before crossing the space for walking. This increases the time drivers have to make eye contact with pedestrians (and stop if

At a protected intersection, drivers approach the foot/cycle path at a 90-degree angle, bringing vulnerable users into view and reducing the chance of collision. (Modacity)

needed). Additionally, by having to traverse the cycle path, there is the biggest opportunity for forgiveness. Should a driver not see the pedestrian at first glance, the extended turning radius and standard 2.5-meter (8-foot) wide cycle path means the driver ultimately has more time and space to brake and avoid a collision.

This becomes all the more important when examining the experience of people with physical limitations. Those with visual impairment use tactile cues, such as textured imprints where the footpath crosses the cycle path and the road, and auditory cues indicating when it is (or isn't) safe to cross. As eye contact is not effective for this segment of the population, they rely on the predictability of these road treatments and the forgiveness of the design to ensure their safety. Paired with an obligatory pedestrian island at the midpoint of the crossing, the entire design of the intersection ensures that people of all ages and abilities can happily navigate these exchanges, trusting their fellow road users to act in a way that is anticipated.

Perhaps the biggest, and arguably most successful trust experiment in Dutch road design is the roundabout. Here, it would appear as though engineers and planners have thrown caution to the wind, removing all traffic lights and relying entirely on collaboration to ensure a continuous flow. The same principles as signalized intersections are employed: 90-degree interaction between drivers and pedestrians/cyclists, shark's teeth, and midcrossing pedestrian islands, with one huge benefit—no one has to wait at a traffic light. Within built-up areas, most roundabouts give priority to pedestrians and cyclists, allowing for their uninterrupted motion, at which some engineers may recoil, thinking it is disrupting the harmonious flow of car traffic. But in actuality, by eliminating the need to come to a complete stop, except when giving way to vulnerable road users, the roundabout actually improves the driving experience. And it has the added bonus of reducing the levels of danger, with the Dutch Institute for Road Safety Research finding roundabouts almost three times safer than a signalized crossing.

In Delft, when a large roundabout was proposed at Delftlandplein in 2009, the average skeptic of the proposed "road diet" would have been justified in worrying that reducing the four-lane road to two would grind car traffic to a halt. The reality couldn't have been further from the truth. The upgrade now enables a continuous flow of the bidirectional cycle lanes to the nearby De Hoven shopping center and new Albert Heijn, along with several high-rise apartment buildings. Drivers travel through the intersection smoothly, having only to stop for (prioritized) cyclists and pedestrians. In fact, the only time any road users must stop is when public transport—namely a tram or bus on the dedicated right-of-way—passes through. Drivers who once experienced a 90-second delay at the former signalized intersection now wait an average of just 10 seconds. At the same time, by eliminating the technological interference, users of the roundabout are now forced to cooperate with each other, reducing the amount of conflicts and collisions.

On his daily trip to and from his new school in Delft, our son has to traverse both a signalized, protected intersection and the aforementioned roundabout. Back in Vancouver, travel through such a major intersection would have caused us a great deal of consternation. Our worries about his safety would likely have forced us to accompany him on his journey. Instead, each morning, we say goodbye and see him on his own way to school, safe in the knowledge that the entire street network—while not completely free of danger—has been designed in a way that means practically everyone is looking out for him. The predictability of his fellow users and the forgiveness of the design reduce the chance of a crash (at least, a "two-sided" crash). At the same time, his experience is helping him learn to have confidence in the people around him, benefiting from a system that builds alliances over rivalries.

All Looking Out for Each Other

Very few would suggest they prefer a competitive society over a collaborative one, but our experience since relocating to the Netherlands has shown how many of these tendencies are baked into our streets. In our previous lives, we were found racing along the Dunsmuir Street protected bike lane in Downtown Vancouver; a 900-meter (3,000-foot) stretch of infrastructure with an astonishing *nine* traffic lights. More often than not, we would fail at multiple attempts to beat the light phasing, which was timed for the flow of motorized traffic, leading to minutes of additional wait time. Looking back, we now realize that the road network was inadvertently shaped to pit each resident against one another. In that scenario, there were no winners.

Our encounters in Delft and across the country have proven there is another way; one where all citizens, regardless of modal choice, can cooperate and trust in each other for everyone's comfort and safety. Sure, modern Dutch culture is built on the polder method, with parties working together instead of in silos, but it is not an anomaly that cannot be replicated. The increased prevalence of Dutch-inspired protected intersections in the UK, Canada, and the United States is proof of that. Certainly the degree of social trust embodied in how people interact on these shared streets is something to which all cities should aspire. In these settings, total strangers act selflessly, picking up fallen bicycles on the footpath because it's just the nice thing to do. And, at the sight of a mother whose child- and grocery-laden *omafiets* (granny

At this Delft intersection, the pedestrians and cyclists have a continuous green light, and motorists must ask for permission to cross the foot and cycle path. (Modacity)

bike) is falling over, they rush to her aid (even if, as in our own case, they don't speak the language). A forgiving and predictable road network cannot build social trust on its own, but by empowering citizens to work together to ensure their security and support, it is a wonderful, unintended consequence.

Chapter 4

The Feminist City

Patriarchy in city planning is not just a failure of society—it is a failure of the imagination.
  — Dorina Pojani

It didn't take long for our family to settle into our new Dutch lives, enjoying the various advantages that come with moving not only to a smaller country but also to a smaller city. After 12 years of living in the heart of one of Vancouver's diverse and vibrant streetcar suburbs, it was nice to be able to slow things down and take time to just enjoy our lives. Vancouver had been a wonderful home; the place where our children grew up, where we first found our passions as urban mobility advocates, and where we fell in love with two-wheeled travel. But after a decade of fighting against the status quo in a car-dominated region of 2.5 million people, and daily struggles with the hostile streets in our community (despite many investments in active travel), it was time to downsize. Delft turned out to be the perfect alternative.

One member of our family, however, was finding the new pace particularly uplifting. Since returning to full-time work in 2016, Melissa had been walking on the delicate tightrope that was working motherhood, balancing her day job with writing a book in her free time, all while caring for and managing the lives of two young children. During that time, Chris worked from home, bearing some of the parental load and creating better equity in the emotional labor. But the fact remained that since the day Coralie was born, Melissa had done most of the care work required to raise a family, from being a stay-at-home mom for several years to working part-time and balancing her career with the active lives of the kids. But within a couple months of moving to Delft, it felt like some of this weight had been lifted, and the contrast between her former life and her current one became stark and celebratory.

It wasn't as though our day-to-day lives had changed that much. The kids were still in school and were soon registered in various extracurricular activities, and we were both working full-time jobs while balancing our consultancy, Modacity, in our spare time. Life's big responsibilities remained the same. Melissa found, however, that little things, compounded over time, could bring a quick shift in emotional well-being.

Her typical workday in Vancouver began with rising and showering, then dragging the kids out of bed, struggling to get them dressed, preparing them for whatever school activities they had that day, assembling their lunch (and, as an afterthought, her own), and then making the half-hour commute to the office—usually by bicycle. Chris would help by walking Coralie and Etienne to school, and picking them up at the end of the day to take them to their extracurriculars, but it was Melissa who knew and managed their schedule. At the end of each workday, she would often stop on the way home to buy ingredients for dinner or lunches the next day. Sometimes, she would collect one of the kids from their activity, often needing to travel well off the most direct and convenient route.

Because of this experience, Melissa made the conscious decision to ease back into work in the Netherlands, waiting until the kids were set up with a regular school routine before launching her career on this side of the Atlantic. There was an understanding that Etienne would require a longer adjustment period when it came to getting to school on his own. But as we quickly discovered, that concern was entirely misplaced. While no one expected that Coralie would want her nerdy parents joining her on the way to her new high school, the speed at which she adapted to managing her own schedule and getting where she needed each day exceeded all expectations.

Instead of needing to look after their daily schedules, and super-vise the children on their daily travels, all while maintaining her own responsibilities, for the first time Melissa was experiencing a level of freedom similar to what she had enjoyed before having children. She was no longer spending all of her time traveling across the city to meet her family's needs; instead, a combination of short trips sprinkled throughout the day afforded her more time to focus on settling into an exciting new career at mobility consultancy Mobycon, experienc-ing her city at a slow pace, and appreciating a flexibility she had long forgotten. Our children's independence in this new mobility landscape, paired with accessibility to every amenity without uncomfortable de-tours, had proved to be just the right combination for a more equitable balance of labor in our household, with Melissa shifting from heavy lifter to biggest benefactor.

It wasn't just the reduced responsibility and increased flexibility she found so comforting. Since the day we decided to start traveling predominantly by bicycle, over 10 years ago, she had become all too familiar with the sensation of isolation in a world dominated by men. Cycling in North America—despite many gains over the years—is still a "boy's club." Even in a city like Vancouver, which was dedicated to building AAA ("all ages and abilities") cycling facilities, it was not uncommon to be one of just a handful of women using the bikeways among dozens of men. Combine that with the fact that she was often one of the only mothers riding with her kids to school, the local shops, and activities each day, and Melissa found herself in a very lonely po-sition. Being the person that she is, she became determined to share her story, and to encourage other women to join her. Gender parity in many countries has a long way to go before it competes with that in the Netherlands, where 56 percent of cyclists are female. Compare that to San Francisco, Barcelona, and London, where females make up just 29 percent, 25 percent, and 37 percent of cyclists, respectively. If these cities are to see a significant modal shift away from private cars, then they need to do far better.

Melissa can't remember exactly when it happened, or what circum-stances may have precipitated it, but soon after our arrival in Delft, she found herself overwhelmed with emotion. Not because she was

No longer the "biking mom," Melissa became one of the thousands of her gender cycling through Delft. It was the completely normal, even boring, thing to do. (Modacity)

homesick, or anxious about the work surrounding the move, but rather, because she wasn't alone anymore. While running errands around Delft on her bike, she passed moms riding with their children, women dressed in skirts and heels riding off to business meetings, teenage girls riding in packs to and from school, young women traveling to their next engineering class at TU Delft (Delft University of Technology), and even grandmothers out for an afternoon ride, before grabbing a coffee together at a local café. Not one or two sprinkled throughout the day, but hundreds of women on bikes.

Instead of standing out as "that woman on the pretty bike dressed in normal clothes," or "Melissa, the biking mom," she was just one of the thousands of her gender moving through the city on bikes. It was the completely normal, even boring, thing to do. Being a "cycling advocate" was a role Melissa had graciously accepted, wanting to make things better not just for her daughter, but for every woman. But here in Delft, there was an incredible lifting that came with not having to be that advocate every time she stepped out the front door. She is now able to channel that boundless energy into her day job, challenging the status quo in the urban planning world, and celebrating what can be achieved when active transportation is made simple, comfortable, and normal; regardless of one's ability or identified gender.

The changes from our Canadian to our Dutch experiences were anticipated to some degree, given what we already knew about the built environment in Delft. But the scale of those changes and the effect on Melissa was unexpected. Of course, there is an inherent calming that occurs when one moves from a large metropolis to a small city of 100,000, but there is something bigger at play on the streets of Delft that allows for these feelings of flexibility and normalcy. The challenge at hand is helping cities on a global scale to recognize the value of these characteristics from a gender equity perspective. In order to do that, however, the male-dominated approach to city building needs to be completely overhauled.

The Problem of the Patriarchal City

"Cities are not natural. We created them." Katrina Johnston-Zimmerman—consultant, director of THINK.urban and adjunct professor at Drexel University—is an urban anthropologist who has dedicated much of her career to exploring the relationship between women and the built environment. She reminds us that, in the early years of civilization, settlements were designed and built holistically and collaboratively. Everyone would have played a supporting role in that process.

"Once we started staying in place it all completely changed," she explains. "After we got past the first earliest cities, which seemed to have been more egalitarian, we moved into a point where we created larger cities and a hierarchy began to take place, with very clear leaders and a distinct segregation of labor." This is the point at which the male-dominated city begins to take shape, when kings, rulers, and clerics decide how cities are built and how people move within them. The Industrial Revolution, or, more accurately, the *auto revolution*, followed. While city structures in and of themselves didn't change that much, their planning structures did. With the invention and adulation of the car, it became apparent that this "tool of the future" needed the space to move and truly become the freedom machine it was purported to be. With no clear policies in place, the people at the top of city management took up the task to plan, build, and manage these new urban environments. They were almost exclusively—as you can probably guess—men.

"At this point, you start to see the emergence of the planner view from 30,000 feet up," describes Johnston-Zimmerman, "where the built environment is simply a series of blocks to move around, without fully understanding the needs of the people within that space." Of course, some of this was no fault of our own. In a world of rapid innovation, there was no clear understanding of how humans would behave when the definitions of space changed. After all, up until this point, cities had remained relatively static in their composition. However, with the decisions being made by the men at the top, and no one asking the people who actually lived in these spaces how they felt, the marginalization that began to take place became inevitable.

Regardless of gender identity, each of us brings our own implicit bias into our approach to work and daily life. In the early part of the twentieth century, as men took up the role as "breadwinner" and women that of "housewife," so too came the separation of work and home. Many families with the means to do so moved farther from the crowded, dirty city center to the quieter outskirts, and the automobile became the reliable mode for men commuting to the city each day. That experience—driving each and every day—translated to their individual experience of the city streets, ultimately affecting their approach to planning those very streets.

"If you look at this through the lens of implicit or explicit bias, if your experience is predominantly driving a car, then you are going to design, plan, and manage for that experience," states Johnston-Zimmerman. One need only look to the legendary feud between Robert Moses—icon of modernist planning—and Jane Jacobs—mother of human-scale planning—to see how planning from a single perspective shapes a landscape for the few and not the many. Funded by the car lobby and a champion of modernity through automobility, Moses was incentivized to build wide roads and highways to make the motor vehicle the easiest and most desirable means of travel. Meanwhile, as a community-minded woman who spent time at street level interacting with neighbors and kids, Jacobs saw the city as a place to gather and stay, perceiving the car as a threat to the social fabric of the city.

The implications of this single-minded focus on automobility in cities went far beyond the expansion of roads and highways. It transformed the entire approach to planning into one that values economic gain over all other aspects of daily life. In the early twentieth century, the Congrès International d'Architecture Moderne—whose membership consisted exclusively of men—coined the four main urban functions: living, working, recreation, and circulation. This highly simplified view valued one thing over all: the *working space*. For the modernists, this translated to locations where paid employment takes place—places of economic activity, with zoning and transport policies that prioritized access to the working space.

Within this framework, care activities were limited to education and health, sport and cultural activities, and publicly provided services. The vast majority of activities needed for the maintenance of daily life—those done predominantly by women, the unpaid caretakers of the family—were excluded from consideration as valuable functions. This has a considerable impact on transport planning, which often fails to appropriately accommodate the needs of individuals performing *care work*.

In her book *Fair Shared Cities: The Impact of Gender Planning in Europe*, Inés Sánchez de Madariaga—professor of urban planning at Universidad Politécnica de Madrid—defines care work as unpaid labor performed by adults for children and dependents, including labor related to household upkeep; that is, work still predominantly performed by women. She acknowledges the need to quantify, assess, and highlight the daily travel associated with care work, coining the term *mobilities of care*.

Although responsibility for care work has shifted dramatically over the past century, finding greater balance between men and women, the division of labor continues to rest largely on the shoulders of women.

In 2002, Harmonised European Time Use Surveys (HETUS) found that in Spain, women between the ages of 20 and 70 spent 4.5 hours per day performing care work, compared to 1.4 for men. Elsewhere in Europe it was similar: in Britain, the difference was 4.1 to 2.2 hours, and in Italy, women were spending four times as much time on care work compared to their male counterparts. Some countries already known for fairer division of labor were more evenly distributed, like Finland, where the difference between genders was just 1.0 hour. In the United States, women conduct an average of 4.0 hours of unpaid work each day, versus 2.4 for men. In most of these countries, this division of labor meant women shouldered the responsibility of childcare when schools closed during the COVID-19 pandemic.

The danger in not considering care work and the trips required to perform it—or *care trips*—in the transportation planning landscape, is that the needs of a significant portion of the population are left unmet. Care trips are often undercounted or uncounted because they don't fall into easily measured, quantifiable definitions. When you think of the average journey to drop kids off at school or daycare, stop at the grocery store, or visit the doctor's office, they are generally less than a kilometer in distance and seldom take longer than 15 minutes. Most travel surveys fail to take these measurements into account due to their brevity, ultimately ignoring entire swaths of mobility patterns. At the same time, care trips are usually arranged in a polygonal spatial pattern—indirect and with multiple stops—covering smaller geographical areas that are closer to home and made on foot or public transport. From a data collection stance, these trips are harder to track than the average, single-purpose commute for employment.

One of the most common characteristics of care trips is they regularly involve a combination of numerous shorter trips and multiple stops, otherwise known as *trip-chaining*. "Our transportation systems are not planned with multiple stops in mind," Johnston-Zimmerman declares. The same surveys that fail to record short trips also frequently overlook trip-chaining, to the detriment of women who are more likely to combine their journeys over a given day. As Sánchez de Madariaga points out, women are more likely than men to stop for errands like groceries and other household-related activities, and twice as likely

When cities fail to consider care trips and trip-chaining in their transportation planning, the needs of a significant portion of the population are unmet. (Modacity)

to pick up and drop off school-aged children. For working parents of children under age 5, trip-chaining occurred for 54 percent of women, compared to 19 percent of men. Additionally, many transportation statistics don't collect information on part-time employment, performed at a greater rate by women. When these systems specifically omit data reflecting the need to make multiple stops conveniently and during nontraditional work hours, especially when looking at noncar travel, women are disproportionately underaccommodated, leading to greater strain and inequity.

Representation and the Feminist City

The simple truth is that decades of underrepresentation in the professions impacting urban design have, in part, led to these inequities on our streets and in our transportation systems. Through her research,

Sánchez de Madariaga equates an overwhelming presence of men in planning professions to an engendered male culture of architecture and city building, ultimately affecting the type of built environment that is designed. In the UK, for example, just 30 percent of workers in the transport sector are women, and 22 percent of architects are women. Only 20 percent of workers in the US transportation sector are female. If implicit or explicit bias is playing a role in how streets and cities are ultimately designed, then increased representation of women in the field will be critical to changing that dynamic.

Johnston-Zimmerman emphatically states, "The biggest thing that has been proven to make a difference is leadership." She points to Iceland, where, following the election of President Vigdís Finnbogadóttir in 1980—the first democratically directly elected female leader of any country—the tide was forever changed, not only in representation of women in political leadership but also for the daily lives of Icelandic women. In the decades that followed, full-time, highly subsidized daycare and nine-month paid parental leave (three months for both parents and the rest to be shared between them) became national law, among countless other policies that improved quality of life for women across the country.

"Even if that woman at the top isn't explicitly saying it, her experiences are enough to think about those areas of society and improve them in some way," says Johnston-Zimmerman. Because women inherently experience the city differently from men, these experiences lead to different levels of leadership, and with a significantly varied approach. From an anthropological viewpoint, it is an intrinsically feminine quality to review, evaluate, ask what's working and what isn't, and then take the necessary measures to correct course.

The question of equity thus comes down to justice: Do people designing cities truly represent those that inhabit them? This traditionally has been—and continues to be—their failing. Despite numerous gains over the years, women still make up a tiny minority of those in positions of leadership and decision making, leading to an unjust situation.

Fair Shared Cities contributor Barbara Zibell—professor of planning theory and the sociology of architecture at Leibniz Universität

Hannover—argues that without spatial justice, as in equity of space for everyone, there can't be social justice. "Social justice is not realizable in the absence of spatial justice: non-fulfillment of the spatial requirements enabling a member of society to live according to a preferred life model, or making this more difficult than it is for others, amounts to a failure of social justice." She highlights that, after decades of research, it is clear that the built environment is far from neutral. A clear gender disadvantage has been built into the fabric of cities because the needs of women have not been given equal consideration: "Improving gender equality in the professions of the built environment is essential to increasing the quality of cities to make them more responsive to everyone's needs."

As the gender landscape continues to evolve to include those who identify as transgender or nonbinary, the argument is made that we can no longer consider a gender-neutral city from a strictly feminist perspective. Johnston-Zimmerman insists, however, that maintaining the title of *Women Planning* rather than adapting it to *Gender Planning* is imperative if we are to truly achieve neutrality in urban design. "When you say 'planning for everyone,' you run the risk of falling back into planning for those implicit or explicit biases," she states. "When you very explicitly say, 'We're creating a gender fair or a feminist city,' that actually calls out your intent and potentially also creates benchmarks and ways to regulate it in a more obvious way."

Oftentimes, feminist planning is a "nice idea," a goal to aim for but not necessarily for creating lasting policy change. This has in fact been the downfall in many European cities following the introduction of *gender mainstreaming* at the United Nations Conference on Women in 1985, and the subsequent Treaty of Amsterdam in 1997. What was set out to integrate equality objectives into all programming objectives was successful in bringing the conversation of feminist perspectives into the planning process, and even inspiring some substantial change. The best example often referred to is Vienna's proactive approach, including the Fauen-Werk-Stadt that created neighborhoods incorporating ideas of a women-focused community, with human-scaled design, safe open spaces, local schools, and other amenities that made life more collaborative and welcoming for women and young families.

Programs popped up across Europe, led by women and focused on improving the urban experience for women, with initial success. But because these departments were often under a larger umbrella of planning, with limited budgets, the work was largely voluntary, and following the 2008 crash, the victims of sweeping budget cuts. Because they were set up as trial programs and not permanent policy change, the ideals of women-focused planning were not integrated into the long-term approach. As departments disappeared, so too did the women advocating for positive change, with representation shrinking, leaving many governments to congratulate themselves on that "nice idea" and moving on. By 2012, just 8 out of the 27 EU states had more than 30 percent representation of women in national parliaments.

"Gender planning is therefore something more," asserts Zibell. "It aims not merely to improve the products of planning, but also to change the processes and the structures. Gender planning is both an indicator and a key action field in the creation of social and spatial justice." Through her ongoing work, she has identified a gendered approach to planning that distinguishes three elements: *Product* involves gendering statistics, equality goals, and planning objectives. *Process* involves equal participation, transparency in decision making, and inclusion of gender expertise. *Structure* involves capacity building within the planning community, institutional change, and integration of the topic into planning policies.

At the end of the day, feminist planning aims to bring dignity to those who have long experienced the city at a disadvantage. "We don't know what a feminist city is because we've never had one," laments Johnston-Zimmerman. From a street-level view, she points to the continuous debate over bike lanes in many North American cities, where perceived low usage gives rise to questions about the justification of their existence, and even their removal. However, it isn't about bike lanes looking as full as car lanes, she argues, but about the access they give to just one person. "What matters is if there is one woman, with a child, who can use that lane to bike that child to school, drop them off safely, happily, and healthily. That alone is enough of a reason to keep that bike lane. If you're not encouraging that with the design, or thinking about her and that personal qualitative experience and quality of

Feminist planning aims to bring dignity to those who have long experienced the city at a disadvantage, by including women from all backgrounds at the table. (Modacity)

life, then you're doing it wrong." For Johnston-Zimmerman and many women living in cities around the world, we've been doing it wrong for generations.

In order to truly achieve gender equity in our built environments, planners and engineers need to step back from that 30,000-foot view and apply a more human-focused approach. One that looks at how each individual experiences the city, how it is letting her down, and what can be done to make her life happier and more comfortable. This includes having women from all backgrounds at the table; professionals and politicians who will provide diverse perspectives to the conversation. "When we look at a city not as a product or as capital," says Johnston-Zimmerman, "then we are thinking of it through the lens of compassion, actual collaboration, and really holistically thinking about your fellow people and their experiences. That is the city that we need to create truly happy, healthy cities." A feminist city is one that is equitable, healthy for everyone, and sustainable.

Planning for a Variety of Users and Journeys

Favoring long-distance, single-purpose commutes over short-distance, multipurpose trips isn't just a concern in motorized transport. It also raises its head in the design of nonmotorized transport networks, explaining why—beyond the presumed (and somewhat simplistic) reason of increased risk aversion—women cycle in far fewer numbers outside the Netherlands. The planning of inclusive and comprehensive networks—that work for a variety of users and journeys—is an art the Dutch have spent decades mastering, but many would be surprised to learn how recent this trial-and-error process began. It wasn't until relocating to Delft that we discovered our new hometown was the very first city in the country to implement a municipal cycling network plan; an eight-year process that began with an enticing approach from the national government, after two high-profile failures, in 1979.

Prior to the 1970s, cycling in the Netherlands was seen largely as a municipal issue, with little-to-no funding or support from the other two levels of government. That changed in 1975, however, when Minister of Transport Tjerk Westerterp announced the funding of two demonstration cycle routes in Tilburg and The Hague, designed to showcase how modern cycling infrastructure could look and feel, with high-quality design, improved detailing, and dedicated space for people on bikes. Both opened in 1977, and both were swiftly declared resounding failures by the local media and community for having failed to attract the hoped-for support and ridership. The route in The Hague became particularly contentious, when local shopkeepers were prosecuted for hiring construction workers to dig up the cycle track in the middle of the night. In their postmortem of these two projects, experts pointed to their lack of cohesion and directness. People declined to use them because they were single corridors, designed in isolation, that forced users to detour several streets out of their way, and navigate different types of confusing and inconsistent infrastructure.

For their third bite at the apple, the Ministry of Public Works selected Delft, a midsized city with a history of good governance, innovative staff, and successful public participation. Resolved to learn their lessons from their prior two defeats, they allocated 27 million guilders (€26.3 million, adjusted for inflation) for the design and construction of an entire network of modern cycling infrastructure. To lead the public engagement process, they hired German sociologist Werner Brög, who surveyed 4,700 households to identify what they felt were the most important physical, financial, and mental barriers to cycling more in their daily lives. In addition to the public, a number of stakeholder organizations were consulted, including the chamber of commerce, Shopkeeper's Federation, Cyclists' Union, traffic safety societies, schools, elderly care homes, and a pedestrian group. One of the key findings was that convenience was key: respondents indicated that they would prefer not to use circuitous routes, even if they were made safer and more comfortable.

To provide for a maximum variety of users and journeys—taking distance, speed, and destination into consideration—City of Delft planners identified not one but *three* cycling networks of varying grid sizes. These networks looked beyond the "normal" 9-to-5 commuting patterns of men, enabling many different types of journeys made by women, especially care trips. The first, called the Urban Network, had a grid mesh of 400 to 600 meters (1,300 to 2,000 feet) and was designed for trip lengths of 2 to 3 kilometers (1.2 to 1.8 miles). The second, the District Network, had a grid mesh of 200 to 300 meters (650 to 1,000 feet) and was designed for trips of 1 to 2 kilometers (0.6 to 1.2 miles). The third, the Neighborhood Network, had a grid mesh of 100 to 150 meters (300 to 500 feet) and was designed for trips of 500 meters to 1 kilometer (1,600 feet to 0.6 miles). In practical terms, the Urban Network could be used to cycle to work, the District Network to cycle to the shop, and the Neighborhood Network to cycle to school.

Delft was lucky enough to have 75 percent of this network already "on the ground" (either through mixed, traffic-calmed access roads or segregated bike lanes on distributor roads), so the fairly limited funding could be applied in a strategic manner. For each of the three network types, barriers and missing links were identified and a solution considered. They included bridges, tunnels, intersection redesigns, specialized traffic lights, and even stretches of missing cycleway. These measures were costed and ranked, based on the number of people they would affect, such that bridging the gaps on the highest-trafficked routes became the highest priority. When the ministerial subsidy was finally exhausted, they had planned for two large tunnels, three cycle bridges, 3 kilometers (1.8 miles) of new connecting cycle links, 6 kilometers (3.7 miles) of one-way streets converted to two-way (traffic-calmed) streets, 5 kilometers (3.1 miles) of new cycle tracks (both separated and on-street), and 10 kilometers (6.2 miles) of cycle tracks resurfaced with new asphalt. To complement these efforts, many crossings and junctions across the network were improved, including approaching lanes, wide positioning lanes, and free-right-turn signs (for cyclists only). Hundreds of new bike racks were distributed across the city, for which car parking spaces were removed.

Passed by the city council in March 1979, the construction phase of the Delft Cycle Plan took five years, and was formally opened with a ribbon-cutting ceremony of the new bicycle underpass beneath the Phoenixstraat railway viaduct on September 19, 1987. It was received with much enthusiasm, likely due to the extensive engagement and the relatively low cost of the improvements. The Fietsersbond (Cyclists' Union), who had been quite critical of the demonstration projects in Tilburg and The Hague, were quite positive about the Delft plan. Most importantly, follow-up surveys—both household and roadside— showed clear quantifiable results. In a few short years, Delft's cycling modal share had grown from 38 to 41 percent, a relative increase of 7 percent. Furthermore, the average travel time improved by 15 percent, while the average distance cycled increased by 7 percent.

Much like the *woonerf* years earlier, Delft's willingness to innovate and experiment changed the way Dutch cities approach street and network design. Later summarized in the CROW (Centrum voor Regelgeving en Onderzoek in de Wegenbouw, or Center for Regulation and Research in Road Construction) *Design Manual for Bicycle Traffic*, the principles that guide this ongoing work likely wouldn't have developed without these successes (and earlier failures). Sadly, their implementation remains a bridge too far for many cities outside the Netherlands, who tend to take a one-size-fits-all approach to network design, to the detriment of everyone not at the planning table.

Take our former home of Vancouver, which has a modest grid of bicycle boulevards that stretch across the city, but these backstreet

Delft's bike networks support many distances and destinations, accommodating complex, multipurpose travel patterns outside the "normal" 9-to-5 commute. (Modacity)

bikeways fail to serve a huge number of potential users and destinations. By nudging its network over from busy shopping streets to quieter residential streets, and spacing the grid at least a kilometer apart, it forces cyclists to take circuitous paths, and makes trip-chaining incredibly difficult. As a result, these routes are mostly used for faster speeds, longer distances, and single-purpose journeys. When you add the fact that there are fewer eyes on these streets, creating social safety concerns, you can appreciate why—despite some safety and comfort improvements—they are still dominated by middle-aged-men-in-Lycra (MAMILs). Until finer-grain routes are built, directly connecting the schools, grocery stores, and doctor's offices, and allowing for multipurpose care trips, women will remain in the minority, regardless of how safe cycling is made.

A Sustainable Future Is a Woman-Led One

The planning and construction of Delft's cycling network provide a perfect example of how our planning approach is very much connected to our freedom and right to the city. Taking the needs of all citizens into account and placing the routes where the vast majority of residents were traveling led to huge success in encouraging cycling for all genders. The streets that we experience today see a continuous stream of people on bicycles from all ages and backgrounds, and most notably, women.

It wasn't long before we started to take this position for granted. Of course, we were smitten with our new home, happily sharing images from our daily trips and weekend adventures on social media. But when given the opportunity to shed the stress of fighting for safe space and representing the cycling culture we wanted to see in Canada, it was easy to fall into a place of contentment. Being just another person on a bike, going with the flow, was an amazing place to find ourselves.

Remember the old adage "You don't know what you have until it's gone." During a trip to Berne, Switzerland, Melissa was reminded of what she had gained in relocating to the Netherlands. In October, our family was invited by Ursula Wyss, the deputy mayor of Berne, to meet with planners and engineers and provide a keynote presentation. A tram city and a UNESCO World Heritage Site, Berne was a delight to wander on foot: quiet, picturesque, and (mostly) accessible.

Part of this visit included a bicycle tour with staff and consultants, and this was where Melissa suddenly recalled what it felt like to stand out again. Despite making some great strides to accommodate cycling in the city, a familiar focus on commuting meant the number of women was distinctly lacking when compared to men, something she pointed out to her hosts almost immediately. There were nods of acknowledgment from the group, but only Deputy Mayor Wyss (the only other woman on the tour) concurred that it was a distinct issue and something that urgently needed to be addressed. Finding herself back in that isolating position was a necessary jolt to evoke Melissa's circumstances back in Vancouver, and those of women in most cities around the world. Being in the company of a woman aggressively leading her city to be better, however, was the inspiration Melissa needed to continue challenging the status quo, even back in the Netherlands.

There is evidence that women's mobility choices are generally more sustainable than men's, and in places where women are leading decision

A more sustainable and equitable mobility system challenges the privileged position of gainfully employed men's mobility patterns as the policy-making norm. (Modacity)

making, their lived experience is having significant, positive impacts. Generations spent making short trips, relying on public transport, and still—to this day—receiving lower incomes, all have led to more sustainable transport decisions. But this is under threat of change; a balancing of gender roles, rather than leading to men making more "green" mobility choices, is leading to women adapting to men's mobility patterns.

Analyzing gendered transport patterns should lead us to question if that template should remain the standard for network design, or if we now have the opportunity to adapt it to a more feminist model. As Sánchez de Madariaga notes in *Fair Shared Cities*, a mobility system both more sustainable and more equitable for everyone challenges the privileged position of gainfully employed men's mobility patterns as the policy-making norm. *Mobilities of care* confront this status quo.

In Dutch cities, many remarkable women are leading the charge to improve their communities. Amsterdam, Rotterdam, and Utrecht are some of many with women leading as mayors, deputy mayors, and mobility managers. We are lucky enough to have two such women in Delft: Mayor Marja van Bijsterveldt and Deputy Mayor for Mobility Martina Huijsmans (both of whom we regularly spot cycling around the city). The future of the Netherlands is looking a little more female. If this helps inspire gender equity here and abroad, not only can the feminist city be realized, but so too can the sustainable and prosperous city.

Chapter 5

The Hearing City

Cities aren't loud. Cars are loud.
— Doug Gordon

The nature of our work has always provided us with the great privilege to travel. Through the work of our consultancy, Modacity, we have traveled across Canada, the United States, Australia, and New Zealand for projects, keynotes, and book launches, mostly in larger cities, such as Montréal, Los Angeles, Melbourne, and Auckland. Living in Canada's third-largest metropolitan area ourselves, we had come to love the buzz and activity of these cosmopolitan areas, even opting to vacation in them, over quieter, off-the-beaten-track destinations—with a few very special exceptions.

Every summer, we would take an escape to some of our favorite natural surroundings: Melissa's family cottage nestled lakeside in the Laurentian mountains in Québec, or on the picturesque Pacific Northwest coastline in Tofino, British Columbia. Despite our passion for discovering new cities, the serenity of existing among the tall trees and nearby waters always served as a much-needed recharge. It was an opportunity to calm all of our senses, but none were more affected than our sense of hearing. Away from the cars, buses, trains, and people, we could enjoy nature's soundtrack, chirping birds, the roar of the ocean, the wind blowing through the trees, all setting us at ease and helping us feel rested and rejuvenated.

Moving to the Netherlands, we were under no misconceptions of the natural beauty we were leaving behind in Canada. In one of Europe's most densely populated countries, escapes like those we had enjoyed would reduce in frequency. The relocation has not changed the need for international travel. Within two months of starting at the Dutch Cycling Embassy, Chris flew to Dover, Delaware, for his first ThinkBike Workshop with the Delaware Department of Transportation. The trip was filled with excitement, networking with his new colleagues while bringing his knowledge and expertise to a group of American traffic engineers looking to make their part of the world better for cycling. The downside was being housed in a hotel nestled between an interstate highway and an eight-lane road, and becoming completely car dependent for a week. It was a total departure from the life he had come to adore, even in Vancouver, of enjoying traffic-calmed neighborhood streets, frequent public transport service, and being able to cycle almost everywhere.

After a rewarding but thoroughly exhausting week, Chris boarded the transatlantic flight back to Amsterdam, and hopped on the direct train from Schiphol Airport, looking forward to returning home to Melissa and the kids. Stepping out of the doors at Delft Station, however, he was overcome with a strong feeling, one he had only experienced in those secluded natural environments back in Canada. He found himself overwhelmed with a sense of calm and contentment.

Most people will agree that there is something truly wonderful about coming home after a long trip. In this moment, however, it wasn't just the act of returning to Delft that caused Chris to pause and take a breath. It was the quiet. After a hectic week of meetings, workshops, and plenty of car travel, walking through the rotating doors at the station was like walking into a wall of silence. Not the deafening kind, but the kind for which many seek to escape the city. He could hear blackbirds singing their night song, the stream of bicycles slowly pedaling by, and the soft chatter of people at a nearby patio. In that moment, Chris gained a new appreciation for how much quieter our new home was, drawing focus to another quality that society has sacrificed in handing its streets over to the automobile: our sense of hearing.

When stepping out of Delft Station, instead of roaring engines, one is greeted by the sound of bicycles, songbirds, church bells, trams, and conversation on nearby terraces. (Modacity)

This feeling was further compounded when, toward the end of our family's first summer in the Netherlands, we resolved to take advantage of the continent-wide train network now at our disposal. We planned escapes on the *Eurostar* to London in August, the *Thalys* to Paris in September, and the *Deutsche Bahn* to Zürich in October. These short breaks were nothing short of magnificent. But in each instance, there was something quite special about returning to Delft. The contrast in experience between arrival and departure couldn't have been starker.

When rolling our suitcases out of St. Pancras, Gare du Nord, and Zürich Central, we were immediately greeted by a wall of noise: engines bellowing in their race to the next traffic light, horns honking in frustration at the abundance of (other) cars, and sirens wailing in pursuit to clean up after the latest crash. This relentless, seemingly unavoidable din had served as background noise to our lives in Vancouver, where our local Skytrain station spit us out at the crossing of two deafening, six-lane roads. It was something that never really registered with us when we were living there. But after six months of savoring the still streets of Delft—and every other city and town in the country, including Amsterdam, The Hague, Rotterdam, and Utrecht—we suddenly felt anxious and distressed, and sought to remove ourselves from the situation as quickly as possible. This was perfectly epitomized when, during a visit to London's Camden Market, we soon found ourselves walking along the quiet waters of Regent's Canal in lieu of the city's historic (but hectic) streets.

What is surprising, however, is that even after growing up in a big city, within weeks of moving to Delft, both Coralie and Etienne made it clear they preferred its serene streets over the energetic cultural centers of Rotterdam and Amsterdam, which they complained were too noisy. This isn't to say that Delft is perfectly serene. The absence of automobiles can make other sources of noise pollution all the more pronounced: the clattering of a garbage truck making its weekly pickup, the squealing of a rotary saw being used for a renovation project, or the periodic *snorfiets* (motorized scooter—not, as Google Translate would have you believe, "mustache bicycle") passing its way down the street. These rolling leaf blowers are a particular nuisance; and while they remain relatively low in numbers, provide quite a shock to the system, especially during the dinner rush, when they are frequently used for deliveries.

This new soundscape we were celebrating didn't just fill us with joy and pleasure. It left us with an immense feeling of calm and relaxation, both inside and outside our house. Which got us wondering: How is noise pollution—and specifically traffic noise—negatively impacting city dwellers around the world? What are the possible solutions for its depletion? How can we adjust our built environments to ensure that everyone enjoys hearing cities, as we do here in the Netherlands?

The World's Most Prevalent Pollutant

While air and water pollution tend to receive the most attention from environmentalists, noise is, in fact, the pollutant that disturbs the greatest number of people in their daily lives. It is a universal stressor, one that stimulates the fight-or-flight response in virtually all animals. An astonishing 65 percent, or 450 million Europeans reside in dwellings exposed to levels above 55 decibels, the amount the World Health Organization (WHO) deems unacceptable. To put that into perspective, an arterial road averages about 80 decibels at ground level, which is perceived as *five times* louder than the recommended intensity per the logarithmic decibel scale.

According to the European Environmental Agency, in 2009, Paris was the third-worst city on the continent for noise pollution, after Bratislava and Warsaw. Fifty-nine percent of Parisians name noise as their biggest nuisance, double those that cite air pollution. Two-thirds of respondents to a French national government survey heard some kind of traffic noise in their home. In New York City, noise is frequently the top complaint to the municipality's 311 helpline. In Rio de Janeiro, despite large-scale poverty, crime, and corruption, 60 percent of all public complaints are related to noise. In Australia, 40 percent of residents are exposed to high traffic noise. In Great Britain, an estimated 12 million people are disturbed daily by traffic noise, 500,000 of whom move to a new house each year because of it. Noise complaints to UK councils have risen fivefold in the past 20 years, where one-fifth of tenants in the London Borough of Greenwich rated traffic noise as being as big a problem as crime. In Moscow, 70 percent of residents live with "unacceptable" noise levels. Even in Norway, which takes the issue fairly seriously, 30 percent of the population lives with noise levels above the WHO standard.

The worst is reserved for regions that arrived a little later to automobility. In India's four major cities, levels regularly average 82 decibels, nearly *six times* the WHO guidance. During rush hour in Karachi, Pakistan, noise levels exceed 140 decibels, louder than a jet airplane taking off at Jinnah International Airport. In Bangkok, Thailand, a city with 10 million people and 5.5 million cars, one-fifth of the population suffers from some kind of hearing loss. In Bangladesh, 98 percent of surveyed residents wanted improved traffic noise control; 91 percent cite car horns as the main cause. In Cairo, Egypt, noise levels average 90 decibels during the day, and seldom drop below 70 decibels at night.

An arterial road averages 80 decibels at ground level, *five times* louder than the intensity level recommended by the World Health Organization. (Modacity)

In Buenos Aires, Argentina, noise on many central thoroughfares exceeds 100 decibels.

An Invisible Threat to Health and Happiness

Researchers are only just beginning to understand how these excessive noise levels affect us physically, emotionally, and socially. According to Dr. Edda Bild, postdoctoral fellow and soundscape researcher at Montréal's McGill University, there is a growing body of research that shows we are failing to fully appreciate the effects constant exposure to noise has on our health and happiness. This is, in part, because the human body adapts to adversity quickly; meaning that, in a short period of time, high noise levels fail to even register. "Often we don't realize we're exposed to noises that are harmful to our health," she explains. "People who live in big cities are used to the churning sounds of passing cars. But just because we don't perceive it, doesn't mean our body isn't having a physiological response to what's happening."

In addition to tinnitus and hearing loss, the human body responds to noise with stress actions, triggering short-, medium-, and long-term symptoms that include increased blood pressure, accelerated heart rate, contraction of muscles, hardening of arteries, indigestion, and insomnia. "There's many years of healthy living we're basically sacrificing because of constant exposure to noise over particular levels," Bild warns. "That leads to higher incidence of certain health problems, particularly cardiovascular issues and sleep disturbances." A 2020 report by the European Environmental Agency estimated that environmental noise contributes to 48,000 new cases of heart disease each year, as well as 12,000 premature deaths on the European continent.

A number of added concerns arise from the sleep disturbances caused by loud living environments: increased awakenings, body movements, environmental insomnia, and use of prescription medication. "Traffic noise has effects over the quality and quantity of sleep, which over time, leads to cardiovascular problems, focus problems, and can lead to obesity," suggests Bild. Even if you reside on a street that's generally quiet, all it takes is a single event—a roaring engine, passing siren, honking horn, pulsing stereo, or wailing car alarm—to wake you up in the night.

Anyone forced to function after a broken night of sleep can attest to its difficulty. The effect is even worse on children, whose bodies are still developing. In 1964, American sociologist Cynthia Deutsch studied children reared in noisy environments and found that—in the classroom—they were less attentive, had lower reading scores, and had difficultly distinguishing important information communicated by their teacher. These problems extend into adulthood, where workplace efficiency suffers from lack of sleep, and fatigue leads to accidents. It is not just sleep loss that decreases employee performance: a 2020 study by the University of Chicago's Joshua Dean concluded that for every noise increase of 10 decibels (a doubling) in the workplace, productivity decreases by 5 percent.

As urban designer and theorist Donald Appleyard discovered in San Francisco, noise pollution dramatically alters how we use and perceive our streets, sidewalks, and public spaces. On all three of the corridors he studied, residents ranked noise as the city's second-most-stressful aspect, after only the danger of traffic. On the street with the heaviest volume, the noise was so severe that many, especially the elderly, were unable to remain objective about other characteristics of their street, as it completely colored the perceptions of their environment. They all demonstrated a similar stress response, causing them to retreat from the outside world. When they did venture out of their homes, they displayed uncharacteristic social behavior: they became less likely to speak to others, assist strangers, remain patient, and demonstrate generosity and more likely to prematurely end conversations, become agitated, disagreeable, and argumentative. This wasn't just caused by the steady drone of traffic; lone offenders (such as motorcycles) also added to feelings of stress and helplessness because there was zero punishment for such conduct, and the driver proceeded with impunity.

Economists are starting to put price tags on phenomena that may have been intuitive but were mostly unquantified. "There are a lot of other associated costs, not just from a humanist perspective, but from a capitalist perspective," asserts Bild. One such cost is the effect of sound sources on real estate prices. This was the conclusion of a 2015 University of Memphis study, in which researchers analyzed the road network and real estate prices in Shelby County, Tennessee. They found that traffic nuisance had a significant negative impact on housing values, with a direct correlation between increasing intensity of traffic volumes and decreasing housing values.

Traffic noise even impacts the natural environment; for example, it has been found to influence the length and pitch of birdsong. In 2018, biologists from George Mason University recorded the vocalizations of various bird species in Rock Creek Park, Washington, DC, and concluded that many were altering their song when adjacent to busy roads. With the din of motor vehicles in the background, birds tended to sing in shorter clusters, with less change in frequency, and a smaller bandwidth, all in an attempt to strain their voices over the noise levels. While it was possible to hear the louder volume of birdsongs over traffic, other birds tended to ignore the songs, and the mating or territorial calls went unheeded. When traffic dropped on the evenings and weekends, the birdsongs returned to normal, and regular social dynamics were restored.

It is perhaps impossible to fully account for all of the monetary costs of traffic noise, but some have tried. In 2007, researchers from a local consultancy, CE Delft, wrote a comprehensive report on the health effects and social costs of traffic noise, and the technical and policy options for reducing road traffic noise in Europe. It estimated the social cost of road traffic noise in the European Union to be at least €38 billion per year, or about 0.4 percent of the total GDP. This staggering amount includes the additional strain on the EU's national health care systems, including resulting medical procedures, prescription medications, and premature deaths. But there was some good news: the same report concluded that, with the right measures in place—including modal shift, speed reduction, quieter tires, and sound barriers—annoyance caused by traffic noise could be cut by 70 percent. And all of these actions are possible and, in some cases, not even difficult to implement. They simply require a better understanding of the origins of traffic noise and the concrete policy steps that are needed to effectively address it.

The Growth of Secondhand Noise

Generally speaking, traffic noise is generated by a combination of two sources: *rolling noise* (created by the tires interacting with the surface of the road) and *propulsion noise* (created by the car's engine, exhaust, transmission, and brakes). While we tend to focus our attention and ire on the latter, the former in fact becomes a car's loudest source of noise at speeds of 55 km/h (35 mph) or greater. For a heavy goods vehicle, the speed is 70 km/h (45 mph) or greater. Thus, on many of the streets throughout our neighborhoods, the friction of rubber on asphalt is actually a car's primary source of noise pollution, an inconvenient truth that won't be changed by the adoption of electric cars. Modest improvements in technology have reduced propulsion noise over the past three decades, but rolling noise is alarmingly trending in the opposite direction, as the automobile industry continues to push out larger and heavier vehicles, which also require wider tires.

At speeds above 55 km/h (35 mph), tire friction on asphalt is a car's primary source of noise pollution, an inconvenient truth that won't be changed by electric cars. (Modacity)

Sadly, in most societies, noise is seen simply as a by-product of growth; an inevitable outcome of increased globalization, mobility, and consumption. This has coincided with a gradual retreat from the public realm, which means many people now pass through, rather than remain in, public space, and see it as the job of others (police officers, garbage collectors, bylaw enforcers, etc.) to look after it. This once shared realm is now often seen as alien territory, and with a lack of ownership, responsibility, or understanding, citizens seldom see the need to modify their behavior while using it. In recent years, this has turned noise pollution into a social justice issue: secondhand noise, like secondhand smoke, is discharged into the environment without consent—from the soundproof cabin of a car—and those of lesser economic means are disproportionately the ones left struggling with its fallout.

The car horn is perhaps the perfect embodiment of the discrepancy between those who create traffic noise and those forced to deal with it. It is a safety device that, in order to be heard clearly at rural speeds and distances, sounds at a deafening 110 decibels (equal to a jackhammer).

The problem, of course, is that it is seldom used to warn others of danger—instead being cathartically applied to express anger, frustration, or impatience, sometimes all at once—and often used in an urban setting. That blast of the horn, in the heat of the moment with very little thought, can scare the daylights out of every pedestrian, cyclist, diner, and resident in a several-hundred-meter radius. But to the driver, as soundproof technology increasingly cocoons the interior of their vehicle in silence, the noise barely registers.

The same is true of the car alarm, another form of protection that has far outlasted its usefulness (if it ever had any). A 2005 report by the New York–based nonprofit Transportation Alternatives concluded that alarms cost the city $400 to $500 million per year in public health costs, lost productivity, decreased property value, and diminished quality of life. It would be one thing if the alarms actually prevented theft, but there is zero evidence that they do. A 1997 analysis of 73 million insurance claims found that cars with alarms show no overall reduction in theft losses. An estimated 95 to 99 percent of all car alarms are false, which is why most American automakers have phased out their factory installation, calling them simply noisemakers.

As Bild and her team of soundscape researchers often preach, it is imperative that cities start dealing with traffic noise on a proactive basis: "We've put ourselves in a corner, but we must start integrating these considerations much earlier when it comes to planning and design." As Marco te Brömmelstroet would attest, that means seeing mobility as more than just a way to get from A to B, and realizing these decisions have consequences. "We tend to think of how efficient traffic infrastructure is, but not how the sound impacts the people around it," she says.

At some point, there may be a message of social responsibility needed to reduce apathy and increase ownership in the public realm. As Bild explains, that involves messaging targeted at the individual driving the car, the person producing the noise: "There's a lot of awareness that needs to be brought to people, not just through the discourse of being a passive victim. But if you own a car, you might be part of the problem." We are a long way from that point, though, as cities must first address traffic noise at its source. That's not a straightforward task.

It has become so pervasive, so intrinsically part of everyday life, that it is difficult to untangle from the urban fabric. We have built streets where, when someone steps out of their home, they don noise-canceling headphones out of necessity, rather than choice. So, if we are to start untangling traffic noise from the city, where is the best place to start?

A Matter of Political Will

As CE Delft researchers concluded in 2007, it is possible to significantly reduce the amount of traffic noise to which urban dwellers are exposed, with the right political will. The concern is that most governments lack the resolve, and if legislation even exists to regulate noise pollution, it has insufficient resources and enforcement policies to make it effective. Many countries—including the United Kingdom, United States, and France—have national noise laws, but these are mostly seen as "suggestions" rather than requirements, due to the lack of resources allocated to implementation and enforcement. So what explains the difference in the sound quality of Dutch cities? They owe their success to a pioneering piece of legislation that is four decades old.

In February 1979, as part of a sweeping environmental and public health protection law, the Netherlands' national government passed the Wet Geluidhinder (Noise Abatement Act), which—among other things—regulated and restricted traffic noise along flow, distributor, and access roads. It prescribed maximum decibel levels within all nearby buildings, depending on their usage and the time of day. Most importantly, it included concrete punishments for noncompliant municipalities, and the resources needed to enforce them. Cities and towns across the country, including Delft, were suddenly faced with two distinct choices. They could push back all new structures several meters from the road edge, which would be completely incompatible with their dense, compact urban form. Or they could nip the problem in the bud, reducing the volume and speed of car traffic to comply with the legislation. Either way, gone were the days of widening roads—at least within built-up areas—since it would make the traffic noise problem worse.

Needless to say, the City of Delft decided to pursue the second direction, and from that point forward, reducing noise pollution was a stated objective of every transport plan the City published. It was, and continues to be, a multipronged effort, that starts with reducing the number of car journeys across the city as a first resort, and constructing noise protection barriers as a last; the former being the most desirable and effective solution and one that brings myriad additional benefits.

The 1970 Traffic Plan and 1979 Cycle Network Plan complement each other in this regard, nudging residents away from the noisy car—at least for short trips—and toward the quieter bicycle. As the low-hanging fruit of any transport plan, these are manageable journeys that occur in large numbers in every country, regardless of size, density, or development pattern. Three-quarters of all journeys in the United Kingdom are under 8 kilometers (5 miles). Half of all journeys in the United States are under 5 kilometers (3 miles). As things currently stand in both countries, the majority of these trips are driven, but could be easily converted to more desirable means, using a similar "carrot and stick" approach.

Of course, traffic circulation plans have the additional benefit of steering motorized traffic away from sensitive areas of the city, which is why you will seldom—if ever—find a café terrace, market square, or public waterway next to a loud and busy road in Delft. Nowhere is this more apparent than along Phoenixstraat, the north-south boulevard home to the central railway station, which was the site of a billion-euro redevelopment project completed in 2014. There, the intention was to reduce transport-related noise, albeit from a slightly different source. For more than 50 years prior, Delft was carved in two by a monstrous (and deafening) elevated railway viaduct. In the early 2000s, the decision was made to bury these tracks in a 2.3-kilometer (1.4-mile) long tunnel; doubling its capacity from two tracks to four, removing the physical barrier that blocked the west side of the city from its core, and muffling the dozens of trains that squealed into the station each hour.

In demolishing the viaduct, engineers suddenly had a width of nearly 60 meters (200 feet) in which to work, and could easily have filled it with six lanes of automobile traffic. Instead, the space was allocated in a far more humane manner, with a dedicated bus- and tramway, a

For 50 years, Delft was carved in two by a large (and loud) rail viaduct. It took a decade to replace it with space for parks, housing, bikes, trams, and a few cars. (Modacity)

canal, landscaping, street trees, and plenty of space for walking, cycling, seating, and dining. The two car lanes—one in each direction—are reserved for vehicles accessing adjacent shops, residences, and underground parking garages. Within these narrow lanes, the traffic seldom exceeds 20 km/h. Decibel levels along this corridor now comply with the Noise Abatement Act, allowing for construction of 1,200 housing units and 50,000 square meters (538,000 square feet) of office space, providing a tangible return on the project's extensive investment.

Which brings up the next most effective tool cities have to tackle traffic noise: reducing the speeds of those cars remaining on the street. It is estimated that a decrease from 50 km/h (30 mph) to 30 km/h (20 mph) would lower the associated noise by 6 decibels, equivalent to cutting the perceived loudness in half. A decrease from 100 km/h (60 mph) to 60 km/h (40 mph) would be the equivalent of cutting the perceived loudness by a factor of four. But of course, these speed limits must be dictated by the design of the street, and not just with a sign. This becomes all the more critical when you consider that the aggressive use of acceleration has been shown to increase noise by up to 6 percent, something that can be addressed only through engineering, not education or enforcement.

One further means to reduce rolling noise is through the use of quieter tires, a move tire manufacturers have successfully (and frustratingly) lobbied against for years. This, despite the fact that adoption of these hushed tires would save European countries an estimated €48 billion in social costs versus their upfront expense of just €1.2 billion. In general, the economic benefits of these kinds of at-source noise reduction measures exceed their costs by as much as *four times*; tariffs that are ultimately absorbed by the vehicle owner, and not the product manufacturer.

There are also mitigation strategies that can be applied alongside at-source measures, but they should only be used to support, not replace them. This is both a matter of effectiveness and economics: the *Dutch Noise Innovation Program* calculated that every decibel removed at-source saves the government €100 million in national expenditure on mitigation measures, such as barriers and insulation.

There is, however, one mitigation measure used widely in the Netherlands, a country on the forefront of the global movement toward quieter asphalt. While certainly not as cost-effective as at-source measures, porous asphalt can reduce rolling noise by as much as 6 decibels (i.e., cut it in half). It has the added safety bonus of reducing aquaplaning and spray, as well as removing pollutants and particulates from the stormwater runoff. Since the early 1980s, double-layer porous asphalt has been used on flow and distributor roads across the country. This includes the few Delft streets designed to permit 50 km/h (30 mph), but since so much of the city's road network consists of 30 km/h (20 mph) access roads, the additional expense is not needed. Some cities may balk at the higher price tag, but porous asphalt is three to ten times more cost-effective than installing noise barriers and soundproof insulation. These mitigation measures have a minor role to play in the worst-affected areas, but must ultimately be seen as a pricey last resort.

Elsewhere in Europe, there are signs that noise pollution is starting to be taken seriously, as governments begin to realize that the costs of intervening pale in comparison to the costs of doing nothing. Passed by the European Commission in 2002, the most prominent of these regulatory frameworks is the European Noise Directive. But that remains a recommendation, not a firm law. Generally speaking, it is something all EU nations tend to respect. It is novel in its approach: asking countries to document their current situation and create benchmarks and action plans; revisiting them every five years. But when it comes to other parts of the world, especially North America, this kind of regulation is simply not done.

Discovering Sounds in the City

If they are to ultimately be successful in their pursuit of more calming cities, officials should be aggressive in reducing motor vehicle volumes and speeds, but they must be mindful about what comes next. "Cars, because of their constant presence, provide a backdrop and the hum of the city," Bild explains. "But what happens when you remove it? You have to fill that silence with something." When cutting off that constant sound, one people are accustomed to, it may not always be preferable. "There can always be an awkward silence," she claims. "It can add to the sense of insecurity and discomfort. When you cut out the noise of the cars, what are you filling that acoustic space with to ensure people feel safe and comfortable?" she asks. This was something almost everyone experienced—if only for a few precious weeks—when the traffic in their city evaporated during the COVID-19 pandemic.

To help fill that acoustic space, Bild and her team started the Sounds in the City project. Funded with a grant from the Canadian government, they aim to bridge the gap between research and practice, and shift the conversation to acknowledge noise as both a challenge and an opportunity. "If we manage to address traffic noise, there are opportunities to fill it with something else," she says. "How do you use sound as a resource to create more welcoming and restorative public spaces?"

These days, it doesn't matter where we travel in the world, we spend much of our time anticipating the soothing soundscape that awaits us outside of Delft Station. Although the front doors drop you onto

Phoenixstraat, a broad and vibrant thoroughfare that cuts through the very heart of the city, the loud hum of motor vehicles is noticeably absent. Instead, one is struck by the sounds normally drowned out by roaring engines: the soft whir of an electric tram gliding by on the rails to Scheveningen, the boisterous laughter of a group of students gathering on a balcony, the chirping of a family of moorhens nesting on the adjacent waterway, and the chorus of bells from the spire of the Nieuwe Kerk (New Church) on the horizon.

Then there is the orchestra of sounds generated by the cascade of passing bicycles: utilitarian machines famously and criminally under-maintained by their owners; years of neglect that create a delightful cacophony of creaks, squeaks, whirs, and rattles. These are the more compassionate and humane street sounds we've grown to adore: the unmistakable "ding-dong" of an oversized brass bell, the subtle clatter-ing of loose bricks under bicycle tires, the clinking beer bottles sitting in someone's front crate, and the joyful tones of a child singing along with their mother. The human-powered traffic fills the huge gap left by the machine-powered traffic, paradoxically bringing the streets to life with sounds that have been all but forgotten elsewhere. It is this para-dox that continues to fascinate and invigorate us: never before have we visited cities that are so serene, yet simultaneously so full of life.

It is fair to say that our sense of hearing is the one that has ben-efited most from the move to Delft, something that extends out of the public and into the private realm. We're fortunate enough to have a large pair of French doors opening from our living/dining room to a second-story terrace. And so, from spring to autumn, from dawn to dusk, we find ourselves throwing them wide open and welcoming the city into our home. Despite being located nearly a kilometer from the Nieuwe Kerk, we clearly register its reliable chimes, at 15-minute intervals, throughout the day and night. The top of the hour seldom goes unnoticed, as a short melody echoes from its 48 bells, followed by alternating gongs with the nearby Oude Kerk (Old Church) to mark the precise hour. Three times per week, and on special occasions like Christmas and Easter, a carillonist climbs the Nieuwe Kerk's tower and performs an hour-long selection of numbers to an audience of 100,000 people (give or take).

The opening night of the Delft Chamber Music Festival, where musicians performed Handel's unmistakable *Music for the Royal Fireworks* for a gathering crowd. (Modacity)

Living in loud cities for much of our lives, birdsong was never something we noticed or particularly cared about. But we now find ourselves transfixed by the variety, musicality, and sheer volume exhibited by the various species that dwell in the trees and bushes and on rooftops around our home, including blackbirds, pigeons, swallows, and even a colony of wild parakeets we spot from time to time (which were, as the story goes, brought from Pakistan as a relic of the city's maritime past).

One summer evening, a few days after returning from London, the two of us stumbled upon an event that perfectly encapsulates what this new sound environment means to us. We were walking into the city center, hand-in-hand, for our regular nightly trip to the grocery store. Unbeknownst to us, it was the opening night of the Delft Chamber Music Festival, an annual event that brings classical music to the streets and squares of the historic city center. We were drawn by the distant sound of music from a nearby canal, and stepped into the most awe-inspiring scene: four wind musicians set up at the edge of the water, enthusiastically performing Handel's unmistakable *Music for the Royal Fireworks* for a gathering crowd.

A large group of tourists, residents, and even a number of small children had gathered, enraptured by every crescendo and staccato. As the musicians played their final dramatic notes, a boat filled with onlookers drifted by, and everyone burst into applause. So often, music is used as something to drown out the relentless noise of the city. But when you realize that cities themselves are not inherently noisy, and in cities that have managed to turn down the volume of the cars, the sounds of a city can take on an entirely different role, even providing a communal experience. A meditative experience. A therapeutic experience. And so, we have learned to cherish the musical moments we share on our rolls and strolls through the streets of Delft: the street organ that navigates the crowds of the Saturday morning market, the accordion player who busks outside the Oude Kerk each Sunday, and the soundtrack that echoes across the city during the annual Delft Blues Festival. These moments benefit both our physical and our mental health, not by our escaping from the city, as is typical, but by immersing ourselves in it.

Chapter 6

The Therapeutic City

It's important to recognize that those factors within the urban environment which increase the risk of mental illness are neither intrinsic nor inevitable aspects of urban living. Instead they are the result of poor planning, design and management, and could be reversed. Which takes us to the next question: could urban living be good for our mental health?
— Andrea Mechelli

I t has become a nightly ritual for the two of us: at the end of each workday, we meet outside Melissa's office to cycle home together, decide what to eat for dinner, and quickly drop our bikes off at the house, before making our way into the city center on foot. After spending our entire lives growing up with the weekly (or even biweekly) "big shop," suddenly we were planning our meals on a daily basis, making the trip to the local grocery store once—and sometimes even twice—per day. In our former lives, we would have thought it wasteful and, quite frankly, bad planning to travel to the shop so often, when all we wanted to do was come home and put our feet up after a stressful day. But with 56 grocery stores within a 30-minute walk of our Delft apartment, we found ourselves buying fresher, more frequently, and in smaller quantities, and our family's health was all the better for it.

A funny thing happened as we adapted to life in a relatively small Dutch city: we actually *craved* that postwork stroll to the grocery store. The act of walking into the city center, passing historic buildings and traveling along streets that see virtually no car traffic, had taken on a therapeutic quality for us both. We could decompress from our day, chat about the highs and lows of our new jobs, about how the kids were adjusting to school, and any number of other things swirling through our heads at that time. This daily journey may serve a particular purpose, but it has also become a cherished way to wrap up our day. That kilometer or so (0.6 mile), 15-minute stroll (each way) provides just enough respite to allow us to leave the stress of the day behind and relax our weary minds before doing it all over again.

It is somewhat ironic that, after moving to a cycling city, we've never done more walking in our lives. Daily strolls are made all the more desirable because the streets of Delft aren't drowning in cars. And we'll be the first to admit that on more than one occasion, when we're laden with heavy bags, we question why it is that we didn't take our bikes. As countless cyclists stream past us on the street, we often joke that we must be the only two people in Delft who chose to walk into the city center.

But these walks are about more than just transportation. They are about our happiness and mental health. Walking along the quiet Hof van Delft neighborhood streets, crossing canals, seeing ducks and ducklings swimming along, and walking past the Oude Kerk as the bells chime are all moments of joy that make the mundane—and altogether necessary—trip to the grocery store all the more memorable.

When we first graduated from Ryerson University and moved to Guelph, Ontario, walking into its quaint center was extremely common for us, inspiring us to buy our first home just the other side of the Speed River. Melissa has fond memories of the first year of Coralie's life, wandering those streets with a stroller, popping into shops and cafés, and building a meaningful bond with the city. When we later relocated to Vancouver, those same values brought us to the Commercial Drive neighborhood, where we spent countless hours walking along the main drag and the tree-lined side streets. But in both instances, despite feeling a strong connection to each place and finding happiness in those walks, they weren't without their stresses.

In Guelph, despite being under a kilometer (0.6 mile) from the downtown core, we had to *twice* cross six lanes of traffic on two of its busiest streets. Even with the center being more destination than thoroughfare, it wasn't uncommon to have cars barreling loudly through,

The act of walking around Delft, passing historic buildings and traveling along streets that see virtually no traffic, has taken on a therapeutic quality for us. (Modacity)

disrupting the enjoyment of our strolls. In Vancouver, although we absolutely adored living in a vibrant community with many independent businesses to support, walking along Commercial Drive was frequently marred by speeding cars, loud honking, and a general feeling of discomfort. The fact that our walk along "The Drive" always began with crossing six lanes of traffic at East Broadway meant each trip started in a noisy, unnerving environment where we often found ourselves racing to make it across the street before the light changed.

In both instances, these walks had a purpose. If we really wanted to relax and decompress, we were forced to leave the community entirely, traveling by car to the green belt around Guelph, or riding our bikes 20 minutes out of our neighborhood to take advantage of Vancouver's extensive waterfront. It's not that these options weren't wonderful— they were—but they couldn't be part of an everyday ritual of relaxation and rejuvenation, without a significant investment of time and energy.

Nowadays, our daily walks in Delft are integral to our mental health.

Whether we need to shop or not, we are certain to dedicate time to wander either the center, our own neighborhood, or the other nearby communities. Because most arterials through the city are no more than two lanes of traffic traveling 50 km/h (30 mph), complemented by prioritization for pedestrians at every crossing, we rarely experience the stress and anxiety we felt in our previous homes. We no longer have that need to escape the way we used to, content to wander aimlessly, and sometimes getting lost—or as lost as one can get in a city of just 24 square kilometers (15 square miles). It is actually quite amazing how we can get caught up in conversation, turning randomly in any direction, going with the flow, and rarely having to pause our discussion to attend to our surroundings.

This isn't to say that we don't want to escape Delft once in a while. A sunny Sunday rarely passes when we don't hop on our bikes and ride the banks of the Schie, into the forest of Delftse Hout to the east, or out among the polders of Delft-Middenland. Although Delft is located in the middle of the Randstad, the country's most populous area, we are still within a stone's throw of ample green space, where we can find reprieve from the city. In just 15 minutes, we can be cycling along seemingly endless paths with nothing but fields around us, experiencing what is specifically referred to as *fietsgeluk* (bicycle happiness). It may not be the Pacific Ocean, but the calm that comes from riding along the pastures can't be overstated.

For one of us, it is that access to cohesive rural cycling routes that has proven incredibly powerful. In March 2020, the offices of the Dutch Cycling Embassy moved from the south side of Delft to the center of Utrecht, a 40-minute train ride away. Although never one to complain about getting to take advantage of the Netherlands' rail network, the loss of Chris's daily ride had a definite impact—but a solvable one. Whenever feeling overwhelmed, he happily hops on his bike, sets his wheels in any direction, and just rides. Traveling through the countryside, he revels in discovering the small neighboring towns and villages, unique bicycle and pedestrian bridges, and getting lost among the polders. With nothing more to focus on than maintaining a steady pace, he can easily put his thoughts aside and enjoy getting what the Dutch call a *frisse neus* (literally, a fresh nose).

Although Delft is located in the middle of the Randstad, the country's most populous area, we are still within a stone's throw of ample green space. (Modacity)

In truth, we have always valued the importance of accessing ways to forget the world around us, and the various stresses that life brings. It has played a key role in how we've chosen each place we've lived. However, until moving to Delft, we were never truly aware of how the high-traffic environment in those places impacted our ability to mentally recharge. In the midst of what many academics and professionals consider a global mental health crisis, we found ourselves living in a place that successfully removed at least one layer of stress that—in a former life—we had just accepted as normal.

How Urban Design Affects Mental Health

When we collectively discuss the global mental health crisis, we often speak as if it is occurring in a vacuum. While the contributing factors are complex and not completely understood, the built environment might be one of the most important and ignored among them. That was the growing realization of urban neuroscientist Robin Mazumder, who, in 2016, was motivated to leave his clinical practice as an occupational therapist in Edmonton, Canada—working on a community mental health team supporting people who were experiencing schizophrenia, bipolar disorder, depression, and anxiety—to pursue a PhD in cognitive neuroscience at the University of Waterloo, studying the impact of urban design on mental health.

Make no mistake, this is a crisis of epidemic proportions, which, according to a 2019 report from the National Alliance on Mental Illness, affects 43.8 million, or one in five American adults. That is 2.4 million (1.1 percent) American adults living with schizophrenia, 6.1 million (2.6 percent) living with bipolar disorder, 16 million (6.9 percent) living with major depression, and 42 million (18.1 percent) living with anxiety disorders. Depression is a particularly devastating condition, affecting 63 percent of US teenagers and 47 percent of millennials, and is the leading cause of disability worldwide. While many of these numbers can be attributed to growing awareness and understanding, and reduced stigma of mental health issues, one cannot ignore the underlying structural conditions we have built into our communities.

With half of all chronic mental illness beginning by the age of 14, and three-quarters by age 24, many factors start at an earlier age than we perhaps realize. Studies have shown that early childhood experiences connect to mental health issues, which becomes troublesome in a society that makes it hard to spend time with your kids at crucial moments in their lives. "We live these chaotic, fast-paced lives where we're constantly working or stuck in traffic," claims Mazumder. "This takes us away from our children who need high-quality interaction at an early age." If the parents are stressed and unable to attend to their child's needs, it has obvious implications.

According to the psychological model of attachment theory, the quality and quantity of emotional bonds we form at an early age influence our neurological development, a model that puts the indoor and backseat generations at a notable disadvantage. "It has been theorized that collectivist societies tend to fare better, because there are a number of caregivers a child can rely on," Mazumder says. "So arguably, neighborhoods where kids are outside, and members have eyes on the street, have a positive impact on the quality of mental health experienced later in life." This is because the responsibility of providing stable attachment figures is distributed evenly within the community; which has a lot do with street design.

"The built environment is perhaps the most detrimental element that affects how people feel," explains Mazumder, who recalls the most common complaint of his patients in Edmonton: "Most of them were terribly lonely, and when I looked at their community to find ways to connect with others, there was a lack of green space, transit wasn't great, and the libraries and public spaces weren't accessible." Human beings are social creatures, and, as Mazumder points out, there's a reason prisons traditionally use social isolation as the harshest form of punishment: "If you think of isolation as a form of punishment, and then examine how a lot of people are isolated by virtue of how their cities are designed, you can draw strong connections between urban design and mental health." With advances in technology, we've become alienated from others limiting our face-to-face interactions. "We stay at home, and when we get out in the world, particularly in cities, it can be a very stressful experience," he says. "The automobile is a large contributor to that."

In addition to engineering social activity out of our daily lives, we've done the same with physical activity, with much of the world's population living in *obesogenic environments*, or places that promote obesity in their residents. Not only has a car been made mandatory for getting from A to B, but the simple acts of going for a walk, jog, or bike ride are made difficult by the threat of motor traffic. This, of course, has negative impacts on both our physical and mental health. "We're social creatures, but we're also mobile creatures," Mazumder explains. "We didn't evolve to be sedentary for such long periods of time." When it comes to our emotional well-being, movement—not laugher—may be the best medicine.

"Exercise facilitates endorphin production, which is implicated in a lot of psychiatric medications," Mazumder explains. As it turns out, moving our bodies—even just a short walk at 5 km/h (3 mph)—creates many of the feel-good chemicals our brain requires. It also moves cortisol through the body: "If you're stressed, moving your body can be a way to help recover. Stress restoration and physical activity are deeply connected." This has been backed by a number of academics, including McMaster University's Jennifer Heisz, who studies the mental health benefits of physical activity. She has found that people who regularly move their body are less likely to develop mental illness. A 2020 study from University College London concluded that sedentary teenagers are more likely than their active peers to suffer from depression. Around the same time, a study from TU Delft (Delft University of Technology) went as far as suggesting that psychiatrists may want to consider prescribing active travel to their patients: "It seems wise to try and stimulate high levels of active travel in the population . . . even as part of therapies to treat depression or other mental health diseases."

These concerns of isolation and inactivity are further exacerbated by the fact that we as a species are spending an unprecedented and overwhelming amount of our lives indoors, with little access to natural sunlight, fresh air, and snow and rain. In the past two centuries, we've gone from 90 percent of the population working outside to less than 20 percent. The average American spends just 7.6 percent of their daily lives outdoors, barely more than the 5.5 percent they spend in a car. Not only has this made us less social and less active, but it has reduced the amount of time we are exposed to nature and the elements, another important preventive measure.

Finding Peace in the Natural World

"There's a lot of correlational research that suggests access to nature has positive mental health effects," claims Mazumder. "People who live near nature are healthier, but we don't know why." There are three major theories that explain this. The first, *stress recovery theory*—developed by Dr. Roger Ulrich of Texas A&M University—suggests that being in nature has positive effects on our mood. This helps to restore cognitive resources and improves our ability to deal with stressful events. After a threatening encounter, nature can recharge our physical and emotional energy.

Kayaking through the old canals in the center of Delft. We may not travel that far, but being on the water has proved incredibly therapeutic for our family. (Modacity)

The second, *attention restoration theory*—developed by Rachel and Stephen Kaplan of the University of Michigan—suggests that the demands of being in a natural space require us to be less hypervigilant than when responding to the threats of an urban space; affording us with a much-needed mental break. "My role as an advocate is to help make urban environments less stressful from the threat of cars," explains Mazumder. "Because if that's one of the things that's implicated in what's good about nature, then we shouldn't have to leave the city to experience it."

The third, *perceptual fluency theory*, suggests that humans need rich, diverse experiences in our daily lives. We consciously create novelty. "The natural structure of nature, from the hues to the luminance to the patterns, is suggested to keep us in an optimal state, and to have restorative effects, because we need that diversity and novelty of experiences," says Mazumder. The visual and experiential complexity of the indoor environment cannot compete with the visual and experiential complexity of the outdoor environment. "We spend so much time on our phones to create new experiences, because our species is geared towards that," he speculates.

Regardless of reason, many cultures have their own traditions of nature therapy. For the Japanese, it is *shinrin-yoku* (forest bathing), a practice that combines a range of exercises in an outdoor environment. This long-standing custom is reflected in the urban design of Tokyo, the single most populated metropolitan area on the planet, of which 14 percent—or 4,177 hectares (10,322 acres)—of the urbanized portion consists of green space. For the Dutch, it is known as *uitwaaien* (out-blowing), which can be thought of as a "wind bath." Embracing the flat, coastal geography where 50 km/h (30 mph) headwinds are the norm, it refers to the act of taking a walk, run, or bike ride in those gale-force conditions. *Uitwaaien* addresses the need for exposure to the elements as a form of mental therapy and self-care, allowing one to clear their mind and feel refreshed.

Unfortunately, with its insatiable demand for asphalt, the car-centered city is incongruous with the presence of nature, insisting on monotony over complexity, and requiring the removal of trees, vegetation, and waterways for real estate dominated by the automobile. In Los Angeles County, for example, no less than half of its land mass is used for the movement and storage of motor vehicles, with surface lots accounting for 261 square kilometers (101 square miles), an area four times bigger than Manhattan. That's a lot of public space that could otherwise be used for public parks. "Car-centric planning becomes utilitarian, and the utility is for car movement," Mazumder declares. Beauty or aesthetic qualities become an afterthought: "The disproportionate investment that's put into car movement and car storage just takes away the resources we have to create beautiful things. The car has sterilized the city and completely removed the human element from it."

"There's a spectrum of urban green space, from fully forested areas where you can't hear cars, to a park beside a busy road," Mazumder describes. The former is needed for the restoration process, but in most cases, this high-quality green space has been pushed to the outskirts of the city. Accessing it therefore requires car ownership—excluding a portion of the population—or a lengthy, inconvenient, and uncomfortable bus or bike ride. Even the low-quality, high-stress green spaces can be difficult to access in many cities, as many parks, beaches, and rivers are severed from the rest of the community by arterial roads, busy motorways, and parking lots.

Learning to "Go with the Flow"

Irrespective of context, under the right conditions, walking and cycling can serve as a form of moving mediation, and unlock an advantageous mental state referred to as "flow." Also known as being "in the zone," *flow* was coined by Hungarian American psychologist Mihály Csíkszentmihályi in 1975, and is characterized by an activity where one is fully immersed in a feeling of energized focus, involvement, and enjoyment. Thus, when one is in flow, there is no sense of time passing. "Occupational therapists really like the concept of flow because it gets to the heart of what we do, which is helping people optimally engage in activities," explains Mazumder. "It's about this matrix of skill and challenge." If you've got high skill and low challenge, you're bored. If you've got low skill and high challenge, you're stressed. When the challenge level meets your skill level, it becomes possible for you to achieve this state of being optimally (fully) engaged.

There is no doubt that streets and cities can be shaped to better facilitate flow. "But if you think about the idea of challenge, one of the biggest things that impedes flow is the threat of cars," Mazumder claims. "You can't get into a flow state when you're constantly worrying about getting hit by a car." The physiological experience produced by the threat of automobiles is not conducive to our well-being. Human beings don't necessarily make good decisions when they're stressed out. "It's literally insane," suggests Mazumder. "We've developed technological advances to live ideal, optimal lives. But we also have to worry about dying all day long. How do we have a conversation about how that's not acceptable?"

One theory around the cause of mental illness, especially schizo-phrenia, posits that there is a threshold of stress people can tolerate before they reach a tipping point. "If you think about the constant stresses we experience, from major life events such as losing a job, we can't do a lot to mitigate those, but we can do something about ambient stresses," suggests Mazumder. In the world of environmental psychol-ogy, *ambient stresses* are low-level, chronic stresses we experience daily, such as noise pollution and speeding cars. Ambient stresses don't pose an immediate threat, but they exist in the background of our cognitive awareness. There are six characteristics of an ambient stress, one of which is *intractability*, or our inability to control it. This actually ampli-fies our experience of the stress, making it more abrasive to our system.

When asked how urban planners can address the global mental health crisis, Mazumder pulls no punches: "Primarily, we need to elim-inate the threat that cars pose. Whether that's through traffic calming or car-free streets, that's the first thing I would target." From there, he points to high-quality infrastructure that buffers against traffic, as well as increasing access to restorative green space, opportunities for social connection, and developing a sense of community and cohesion.

Mazumder, who identifies as a racialized person, also believes it is important to recognize that good infrastructure and access to nature alone won't mitigate the stress of the city for everyone. He highlights that Black, Indigenous, and people of color also have to contend with police surveillance and racism in these spaces, which can cancel out the restorative effects. Psychologist Dr. Rodney Clark concludes that chronic racial stress results in prolonged activation of the sympathetic nervous system, which has implications on both mental and physical health. Accordingly, equity also needs to be prioritized, alongside the push for better urban design. "This requires a multi-pronged approach; one that recognizes the nuances of the urban experience," suggests Mazumder. But when it comes to addressing the problems caused by the automobile, how realistic is removing the threat of cars from cit-ies? In digging not too far back into Delft's history, to the turn of the twenty-first century, we discovered the answer. And it didn't happen without a fight.

Eliminating the Threat of Cars from the City

After curbing traffic for the better part of 30 years, in 1998, Delft found itself at a critical crossroads. Surprisingly, while the 1970 Traffic Plan prevented automobiles from cutting directly across the city center—the 800-year-old core that was fortressed, gated, and moated until the 1830s—they could still comfortably enter, and then park along a number of canals or in many of the public squares. In the first transport plan after the Second World War, all of these squares were designated as parking lots. With a left-of-center coalition narrowly in charge of municipal politics (a typical "polder model" consisting of the Green, Student, and Labor Parties who controlled 19 of 37 seats), led by GroenLinks (Green Left) alderman Rik Grashoff, the local transport discussion shifted, for the first time, from safety to *livability*, and the idea of establishing an *autoluwe binnenstad* (low-car city center) emerged.

In response to those shifting priorities, a new transportation policy was developed by staff, one that sought to remove nearly all of the automobiles from the economic heart of the city, reserving it solely for pedestrians, cyclists, and buses. With the threat of automobiles largely removed, these three modes could mix quite comfortably, without the need for segregated infrastructure. The car-lined canals and car-choked public plazas, the latter of which were historically used for livestock, flower, and produce markets, would be restored to their former glory. Many of these "lost" parking spaces would be replaced in three newly built underground and multistory garages, strategically located around the perimeter of the city center. Drivers would, of course, be welcome downtown, but their modal choice could no longer impede on the enjoyment of residents and visitors. If they wanted to bring their car to shop or dine, they would have to leave it outside, and enter on foot.

The majority of this new mobility plan was implemented with little to no controversy, a testament to years of providing viable alternatives to the car, but there was one notable exception. When it came to the final piece of the low-car puzzle, a heated and heavily contested disagreement arose around Delft's Markt, the beautiful central square flanked by the 400-year-old Stadhuis (City Hall), the 600-year-old

Nieuwe Kerk (New Church), and about 40 different restaurants, cafés, and retailers. Despite being the main tourist destination in the city, and the site of the Dutch royal family's private crypt, it bizarrely doubled as a parking lot, with a peak capacity of 150 automobiles. The wasted space was one thing, but staff estimated that, at any given time, several hundred other vehicles roamed the narrow streets searching for a spot. If they were to ultimately succeed in removing the threat of moving cars, they would also have to succeed in extracting much of the parking.

But in 2003, when it came time to convert this space for cars into a space for people, the adjacent business owners vehemently opposed the move. "We're not the Mediterranean," seems like a strange refrain in the present-day Netherlands, but at the time, the City's proposal was met with a great deal of skepticism. Sure, France, Spain, and Italy had walking and terrace-sitting cultures, but until then, critics claimed that the Dutch traditionally did not live outside—at least year-round—due to their harsh climate. Restaurateurs feared that the patios might be packed in the summer months, but they would quickly empty out during the wet and windy winters. So, rather than drag them along unwillingly, municipal staff organized a summit of over 200 stakeholders, and hatched out a clever compromise. They planned to bring them along, and demonstrate that—with the right bold moves—terrace cultures could be created that could be rather lucrative for their bottom line.

They pitched a six-month pilot project to a handful of retailers on the north side of the square, temporarily trading a few car parking spaces for a few dozen tables, and offering to assess the impacts on the levels of commerce. If the levels dropped for whatever reason, the planners could return to the status quo. No harm, no foul. However, these terraces proved immensely popular, regardless of the weather conditions, showing that "Mediterranean culture" could be imported to the North Sea. Retractable awnings, propane heaters, and wool blankets were provided to shelter customers from the elements and augment the feeling of *gezelligheid* (coziness).

Soon, individual restaurants were turning over a few hundred euros per table per night, and the value of outdoor commerce became abundantly clear to everyone. Word spread up and down the Markt, and the remaining business owners approached the City to demand

Once the site of a heated disagreement around surface car parking, Delft's Markt square is now bustling with commerce, community, and connection. (Modacity)

the same agreement. The rest is history, and Delft's figurative "living room" became permanently car free. Ironically, one of the first events to take advantage of the fully reclaimed square in the spring of 2004 was the Delftse Autosalon (Delft Motor Show); a now-annual event that attracts automotive dealerships and 10,000 visitors from across the region. Today the square is bustling with commerce, community, and connection: tourists taking selfies in front of the New Church, children running around and playing tag, and patrons packed on the patios for dinner and drinks. It is difficult to believe that this space was jammed with parked cars just over 15 years ago.

Hearing this story, we couldn't help but think that our former home of Vancouver currently sits at a similar crossroads. Having successfully promoted alternatives to the car for years, a number of popular precincts beg for a "low-car" treatment, including Gastown, Stanley Park, and Granville Island. In each case, thousands of residents and visitors flood the narrow footpaths and tight terraces on a daily basis, only to have their enjoyment of the space stifled by a handful of motor vehicles that are either passing through or looking for a place to park. Sadly, many politicians, media, and business leaders conflate unrestricted automobile access with economic vitality, and they defend the status quo with the familiar refrain of "We're not the Netherlands." But as Delft proves, neither was the Netherlands, as recently as 2004.

Whereas retractable bollards were initially used to keep unwanted cars out of the center, nowadays, a series of video cameras serve as the gatekeepers of Delft's *autoluwe binnenstad.* Anyone wanting to enter the center with a motor vehicle—whether freight, service, or resident—must purchase a daily, monthly, or yearly permit on the City's website. Free exemptions are granted for those with mobility impairments. Everyone else must park at one of the paid facilities on the outskirts and enter on foot. Those who don't do so risk having their license plate recorded, and a hefty fine sent in the mail. Contrary to those skeptics at the turn of the century, day or night, rain or shine, most of Delft's streets and squares are bustling with people; they are picking up fruits and veggies from the morning market, savoring a pilsner on one of the many busy terraces, or simply out for a leisurely walk or bike ride.

Despite the success of this policy, some of Delft's historic canals remain lined with parked vehicles, owned mainly by permit-carrying residents, but no less of an eyesore. In areas where local cars can still move freely, pedestrians find themselves squeezing into any available space to allow them to pass, detracting from what would be an otherwise very pleasant walk through the city. From a structural point of view, many of Delft's bridges date back to the 1800s (or earlier), and were simply not built to handle the weight of today's cars, let alone that of the average delivery truck. These days, it is not uncommon to find canal crossings taken apart brick by brick, simply to be stabilized and reinforced so as to avoid crumbling.

City Hall has been closely monitoring all of this, understanding that the work toward a more prosperous and accessible center is never actually complete. Their next step is the development of the Delft Mobiliteitsprogramma 2040 (Delft Mobility Program 2040). The bold plan builds upon the initial improvements made in the early 2000s and involves the removal of thousands of additional parking spaces from along these canals. Within the next 20 years, this policy will be

Video cameras serve as the gatekeepers of Delft's "low-car" center. Anyone entering with a motor vehicle must acquire a permit on the City's website. (Modacity)

an integral blueprint, as the city marches from a low-car center to an *autovrij* (car-free) one.

Connecting to Nature on Foot, Bike, or Boat

As we sat down in March 2020 to start writing this book, life as we knew it came to a halt—almost overnight. As countries everywhere began imposing lockdown measures to mitigate the damage of the COVID-19 pandemic, our family suddenly found ourselves constantly in each other's presence. The children launched directly into digital lessons from their schools, while Mom and Dad turned their kitchen table into a home office. Like billions around the world, the change of routine combined with an overwhelming sense of uncertainty, lack of control, and feelings of isolation took their toll very quickly. As we went into triage mode, trying to ensure that our children understood what was going on, while doing what we could to maintain some normalcy for them, we could feel our own mental stability slipping.

In this moment, we became incredibly grateful to find ourselves in the cozy confines of Delft. Activities we had grown to love in our first year became our medicine for sanity: meanderings in the city center, and getting lost on the streets in our neighborhood helped us briefly forget about what was happening around us, not to mention giving us much needed time away from our children (as any parent can attest). However, with guidance in place to ensure social distancing of 1.5 meters (5 feet), and most residents also looking for outdoor reprieve, it sometimes proved difficult to maintain physical distance during daytime walks or rides.

So we adjusted, taking our daily trips in the later evening, not only enjoying fewer pedestrians and cyclists on the streets but also the immense calm and quiet. As stated earlier, with traffic-calmed streets, we experienced much less traffic noise in Delft than in cities where we have lived before. But during the COVID-19 crisis, that was amplified, as most people stayed home and cars all but disappeared. These nightly travels became our therapy, finding peace in the sounds of birds, leaves rustling in the breeze, or—on longer rides into the countryside—bathing ourselves in the warmth of the setting sun. Truly, the opportunity for *uitwaaien*, even as measures lifted three months later, was integral in the quality of our mental health.

It wasn't just us. Coralie and Etienne proved remarkably resilient throughout this period. We're not sure why, but it might have had to do with their not having to physically attend school, and daily lessons being half of what they were in more normal circumstances, with much of the remaining time filled with video games. It became clear to us, though, when they had been stuck inside for too long. In those moments, when we were buried under Zoom meetings and project deadlines, the ability to send our children out for their own walks could never be undervalued.

Each day, once they completed and submitted their schoolwork, they set out onto Delft's streets for some fresh air, some exercise, and some time to themselves. Coralie started walking over to the nearby Wilhelminapark with a blanket and her sketchbook, and taking time in nature to relax and draw. She even managed to find a small communal green space tucked away between the rows of houses in our neighborhood, which she refused to share, thinking of it as her secret hideaway.

Etienne, on the other hand, took to walking into the city center to execute our latest family project: capturing photos of the many cats of Delft. Not long after our arrival, we became acutely aware of the sheer number of cats on the streets. In a place where the threat of cars is so low, it is common for the family cat to roam freely outdoors. Families like ours, where our precious tuxedo cat, Mittens, stays indoors or within the confines of our *dakterras* (roof terrace), are the exception and not the rule. In response, Coralie started the "Cats of Delft" Instagram account to share pictures of the many felines we encountered walking through the city, which Etienne then took over, using his COVID-19 walks to hunt for kitties to photograph.

Living in a place with low traffic meant that as parents, we never once worried for our children's safety. Their mental health breaks didn't negatively affect our own mental health, and that fact is incredibly valuable, not just in times of a global pandemic but on a day-to-day basis as well. Parents inherently worry about their children; it's normal behavior. Choosing a city that has afforded them incredible freedom and autonomy by creating safe places to travel has taken away one level of stress for them and for us. Coralie and Etienne can enjoy time to themselves, and we in turn can relax in the comfort of knowing they're relatively safe and happy.

More recently, lockdown activities have transformed into daily rituals, but of course we always look for new ways to "escape." After countless strolls along Delft's canals and the Schie River, we decided it was time to take our mode of travel to the water. In May 2020, using money she received as a gift for her 40th birthday, Melissa purchased two inflatable double kayaks and, in her words, "We've gone from being bike people to being boat people." As summer crept in, we would take the boats out to the canal on Buitenwatersloot, just 200 meters (656 feet) from our front door, and paddle as a family through the old canals of the center, or west toward the countryside. We may not travel that far, and have laughed as we struggle to paddle in a straight line, but being on the water has proved incredibly therapeutic.

Having that connection to nature—whether on foot, on a bike, or in

a boat—has been key to our happiness, and we recognize how the effortless access we now enjoy plays a huge role in our overall satisfaction
and contentment. We certainly made use of what was available to us in
the cities we lived in before, but there is something to be said about not
having to go too far to find that level of enjoyment. Certainly, through
difficult circumstances, it proved vital in maintaining both our physical and mental well-being. And it will continue to do so regardless
of external factors. Delft's quiet, cobbled streets, historic architecture,
stretches of green pastures and forests, and still sparkling canals are all
ingredients in the recipe of improved mental health.

Chapter 7

The Accessible City

People aren't disabled. The environment they live in is.
— Karel Dollekens

Over many years of advocacy work, we have witnessed the role the humble bicycle can play in granting autonomy to virtually everyone, starting at the earliest age, from watching our own children grow up on two wheels, to seeing countless cities around us evolve to get more people riding more often. A central goal for many of these cities developing networks of infrastructure is that it be for "all ages and abilities." But the reality on streets and in public spaces often falls short of that goal. High curb heights, insufficient curb cuts, narrow sidewalks and bike lanes, and a lack of storage facilities let people down, especially those living with physical disabilities.

Although we are lucky enough to consider ourselves nondisabled, we are acutely aware that like everyone, we may experience disability at some point in our lives. Furthermore, given the increasing populations of older citizens and more years lived with multiple chronic conditions, disabilities may become more prevalent. Countless conversations with people living with chronic illnesses that vary, such as rheumatoid arthritis, have helped us to appreciate that disabled and nondisabled people are not two entirely distinct and fixed groups. We saw firsthand in North America that cities needed to do better to help people maintain their independent mobility.

So when we traveled to the Netherlands for the first time in 2016 and saw how this *fietsparadijs* (bicycle paradise) was also allowing people with handcycles, tricycles, tandems, and a variety of other adapted devices to move freely and independently, we were amazed. What was built to make cycling easier was also making life easier for those historically underserved in the transport world. Our new hometown of Delft is no exception. On every outing, we see people of all ability levels walking, scooting, and cycling along the *fietspaden* (bicycle paths) and *fietsstraten* (bicycle streets).

Maya van der Does-Levi is one of those people. A Tel Aviv native, and Delft resident since 2007, Maya has multiple sclerosis, an immune-mediated disease that disrupts the flow of information within the brain, and between it and the body. For Maya, this has meant living with a progressive reduction of physical mobility since being diagnosed in 2003. "I know what it is to be completely enabled and I know what it is to have some disabilities," she states. After living a large portion of her life completely able-bodied, she has experienced the gradual loss of physical ability that—in the earlier stages of the disease—forced her to walk using the help of Nordic sticks. As a self-professed stubborn person, Maya was not willing to forgo her freedom easily, despite frequent falls, even with the support of walking sticks.

This served her well until the summer of 2018, when Maya experienced a relapse that left her nearly immobile. Until then, while independent travel had not come without discomfort, she was still that—independent. Her deterioration left her wheelchair-bound, relying on others to help her get around. "It was very difficult. That was the first time in my life I really felt the physical disability of my illness." Reflecting on that point in time, Maya admits she hit rock bottom, overwhelmed by feelings of helplessness, mainly due to a loss of mobility. In the early days of that relapse, she borrowed a heavy wheelchair and was pushed around by friends and family. "No matter whether you are traveling by car or walking, it's really not nice," she explains. "When you go somewhere and the people you are with want to step away to do something, you are just 'parked' there. It's pretty unpleasant."

This incident turned out to be a blessing in disguise for Maya. Unwilling to simply sit back and let her disease dictate her mobility for the rest of her life, she started rehabilitation to build enough strength to walk again, even with aids like crutches. She was married to a Dutch man, and they loved being active together; losing that ease to go out together motivated Maya to discover new activities. She started horseback riding and sailing lessons, and purchased a handcycle to tour the countryside with her family. At the same time, day-to-day travel remained immensely challenging. "Mobility is definitely something that is close to my heart, because I always want to maintain my independence as much as possible," she emphasized. With children then aged 6 and 9, she needed to be portable. With financial support from the Municipality of Delft—which provides subsidized mobility devices to all of its residents that require them—she purchased a *scootmobiel*, a three- or four-wheeled motorized scooter specifically designed for people with limited mobility. Maya remembers not being too enthused by it at first, but as it turns out, purchasing that three-wheeled *scootmobiel* was the key to unlocking her unlimited mobility potential, and changing how she understood transportation.

"When I got the *scootmobiel*, I discovered how amazing the infrastructure is here even for people like me that cannot bike," Maya declares. Because walking had long been challenging for her, she was already occasionally using Delft's cycling infrastructure, with its wide, smooth, relatively flat conditions. On her *scootmobiel*, it was clear that many of the city's narrower sidewalks, especially in the city center, were inaccessible. The ubiquitous red paths and bicycle streets provided the perfect conditions for traveling safely throughout her city. She quickly adapted to her new mode of independent transport, incorporating it into her daily routines.

Maya has a full and diverse life, and her schedule as a mother of two is not too different from that of more physically able parents. In the mornings and afternoons, she drops off and picks up her daughters by *scootmobiel* from school, friends' homes, and their various extracurricular activities. She takes full advantage of delivery services for her larger grocery needs, using her *scootmobiel* for smaller purchases that don't overwhelm the capacity of the device. Additionally, she travels by

Although Maya doesn't cycle for transport, Delft's ubiquitous red paths and bicycle streets provide the perfect conditions for traveling safely throughout her city. (Modacity)

scootmobiel to the gym and her physiotherapy appointments. What is perhaps most impressive is that Maya uses her *scootmobiel* to commute to and from her newest vocation—completing her bachelor's degree at The Hague University of Applied Sciences to become a registered dietician.

With a battery range of about 35 kilometers (20 miles), Maya comfortably travels the 15-kilometer, 40-minute journey to class along the scenic Schie, happily making use of the *fietsstraten* on each side of the river. While the trip satisfies her love of accessing nature, being able to make it on her own three wheels is about more than simply enjoying a waterfront route: "For any person in this world, with or without a disability, but especially with a disability, the most important thing is to be able to be independent," she states emphatically. Earlier in her life, Maya held a driver's license. But due to the degenerative nature of her illness, it was eventually taken away, leaving her to find other means of transport to maintain her self-determination. Her *scootmobiel* does exactly that, with infrastructure and traffic calming creating an environment that empowers her to keep her independence.

There is, of course, one inevitable question: what happens when Maya, someone with limited independent mobility, needs to travel outside the range of her *scootmobiel*? To this, she emphasizes the importance of having an entire structure in place: "It's important to have a system. You can design something with great bike lanes, but with no investment in places to park and charge, or ways to get outside your battery range, the system doesn't work as well as it should." This is where accessible public transport complements the active travel network at street level.

Maya is the first to admit that the bus, tram, and rail networks don't work for her. The hassle of having to call an hour ahead to ensure staff are on the platform to put a ramp in place is incredibly cumbersome. Not to mention that this works only when all the puzzle pieces are in place. An unavailable ramp or out-of-service elevator makes the trip impossible. To enable travel outside the range of her *scootmobiel*, Maya uses the subsidized RegioTaxi—a reservable bus service that caters specifically to people with disabilities. For about the cost of a trip on regular public transport, Maya can go nearly anywhere within the region with her *scootmobiel* because it enables her to access the RegioTaxi service. Taking regular public transport or a car can prove quite challenging, due to the size and weight of the device. Substitution of her *scootmobiel* for a folding wheelchair significantly decreases her comfort. It should not be a sacrifice that she—or anyone—has to make. "RegioTaxi enables people with disabilities to broaden their range," Maya points out. "It helps people make trips where otherwise they would be stuck at home. It's amazing. I love to sit and watch fellow passengers and enjoy the scenery."

Although a national program, RegioTaxi falls under municipal jurisdiction and funding, unless it is used for schooling or work, when it becomes the responsibility of the employee's insurance agency. For other journeys, such as going on vacation, Maya turns to Valys, a service for travelers with reduced mobility who want to make social-recreational trips outside their region. Using her annually allocated budget from the municipality, and sometimes supplementing it herself, Valys allows Maya the ability to travel anywhere in the country with her family without having to worry about how to find space for everything she needs. "When you sit down and look at it, on an average vacation I need to take my *scootmobiel*, my handcycle—and that also means my wheelchair—and this apart from my and everyone else's luggage," she explains. "It's really amazing because I just order it, and they bring you with all your stuff! I can vacation with my family without having to buy a specialized vehicle."

Speaking to Maya, it is obvious that—thanks to a combination of factors—she can maintain her freedom of mobility relatively easily. She insists that her quality of life, in spite of her illness, has been sustained—if not improved—by the ability to travel almost anywhere with her *scootmobiel*. That also inspired her choice of profession: "It took some time to decide what I wanted to do, and I feel with my personal experience, I can contribute to the well-being and quality of life of others as a dietician."

An active lifestyle is central to that: "I am very much someone who advocates for people to be active, especially those with health conditions," she explains, pointing to the Dutch concept of *zorggerelateerde preventie* (care-related prevention). "This is my mission." Although using a *scootmobiel* doesn't necessarily increase physical activity for disabled people, the device plays a critical role in improving their mental health. "A *scootmobiel* exponentially increases not just mobility but also social connection," she reveals. "Psychologically, it is amazing. I meet people in the city all the time because I can move around in my *scootmobiel*, and I love that!"

For Maya, and many like her in the Netherlands, these factors—access to mobility devices, an infrastructure network, and supplementary public transport to broaden the range—work together to ensure that physical limitations don't mean being completely cut off from the world. Maya feels that the strongest link in the chain is the bike infrastructure: "The infrastructure for the bicycles is empowering, not just for cyclists, but also for people with disability. For me, it has been emancipating."

This is so often overlooked by urban and transport planners. A person's access to the streets and city around them means more than just being independently mobile. It means being connected to the environment and to neighbors. Without that, many people are actively excluded from society—a group that may one day include each and every one of us.

Challenging Disabling Environments

"Every person is on a continuum from strong to weak, from tired to energized, from depressed to exuberant, and from pain-free to experiencing chronic pain," explains Dr. Bridget Burdett, a principal researcher at MRCagney—a transport consultancy based in Auckland, New Zealand. She has dedicated much of her career to improving equity and well-being, including promoting the needs of people with disabilities. Her work is aimed at addressing and correcting the root causes of disabling environments, which can be defined as places that exclude people, or make their participation more difficult or more expensive compared to that of others.

When car-centric environments are viewed through this lens, it becomes clear that they do not benefit everyone equally. Car-first planning, at its essence, perpetuates the idea that transport networks are provided for those with motor vehicles, who are therefore freely mobile with their choices. It is exclusionary, overlooking the needs of portions of the population: children, the elderly, those living on a limited income, and, importantly, individuals with a physical disability.

For people advocating for the reduction of space allocated to automobiles in cities, this is a challenging dichotomy. Many members of the public are under the false impression that those with disabilities rely exclusively on cars to get around, often using this as an argument to maintain the status quo. Proposing to remove car lanes or parking is (either honestly or dishonestly) equated to removing access. In her 2008 paper "Transport: Challenging Disabling Environments," Rachel Aldred highlights how in London, 72 percent of car trips are under 8 kilometers (5 miles) in length. This distance is easily traveled by bike or vehicles of similar speed, such as electric scooters. "However, like the Department of Transport's handbooks, the Disabled Persons Transport Advisory Committee prioritizes private cars, stating that for many disabled people, private cars are the only form of accessible transport, and that restrictions on car use are negative for disabled people," she writes.

In fact, the opposite is true. According to Aldred, 60 percent of disabled persons in the UK are without access to a household car, compared to 27 percent of the general population. "Car-centric planning means we have fewer choices," Burdett explains. "Cars are very inefficient, so by necessity destinations have spread out, and that has led to a dispersal of opportunities, creating a disconnect between where people live and where they want to go." This makes reaching a destination incredibly challenging, particularly for the disabled. They may not be able to drive, and—as in Maya's case—can't rely on public transport. Never mind accounting for trip-chaining and combining multiple stops. "This is how disabling environments are created; they are not comfortable, attractive, or easy for all people to access, and don't treat everybody the same in respect to those attributes," says Burdett.

Most Western cities are designed to maximize the ease of automobile travel, with every other mode forced to adapt around it. In his book *Disability and the City*, Rob Imrie explains this through the presocial model of disability: "Because the built environment facilitates access for most people, it should be possible for disabled people to adapt their behavior to the environmental constraints they encounter." In the United States, this has led to an approach that largely views disabled people as a group to be "dealt with" rather than accommodated; something that "costs" money, as part of the welfare state. There is little emphasis on or consideration of the importance of preserving the autonomy and civil rights of the individual person.

Once again, the automobile-centered ideals of modernism left their mark, centered around ableist ideas embodied by Le Corbusier: "All men have the same organism, the same functions . . . the same needs." He and others viewed the separation of home, work, industrial spaces, and parks as a sign of progress. This, however, was predicated on individual mobility as a means to access each of these places, leaving anyone with limited means or mobility out of the equation.

Dr. Burdett identifies an important result of this modernist model: "We talk about travel time costs for cars, but we don't talk about the

Electric tricycles are increasingly popular, not just for people with physical impairments but also those unable to balance on a two-wheeled bicycle. (Modacity)

travel time costs for people, and especially disabled people who experience higher costs because their environment is disabling." She points to the diversions and accommodations most disabled individuals have to make for every trip—and that's just when the weather is pleasant. Ableist thinking presumes these people will have an adapted motor vehicle that makes these trips easier. The truth is that most do not, due in large part to the prohibitive expense of such vehicles. Since most cars are designed for a "standard" body—namely male and an average height of 170 centimeters (66 inches)—they are not suited for those with mobility impairments. Adjusting these vehicles is incredibly costly, and the expense increases because many insurers regard disabled people as a higher risk and raise their premiums as a result.

The presumption that all people are created equal is a slippery slope at the best of times, and transport planning is no different. Car dominance reinforces the notion that either you find a way to fit the mold or you get out of the way. Dr. Burdett argues that the best way to progress from such thinking to a more inclusive and equitable space is to create policies that include the principles of universal access, something she is helping to do in New Zealand. The three core principles are that the design needs to be *safe*, to be *obvious*, and to provide *step-free choices*. "Our goal is to create a guideline that is easy to incorporate," she details. "Simplifying it provides a nice lens for professionals to think about what to do rather than focusing on what not to do."

As with Maya's lived experience in Delft, Dr. Burdett points to the potential to solve many accessibility issues with bike lanes. Through their implementation, more space is created for walking, cycling, and mobility aids. "In our communities, we need to design in a way that reclaims space from cars and provides space for people who need it." When that space is incorporated with elements such as quality wayfinding, generous footpaths, and plentiful curb cuts, it makes transport access easier, regardless of ability. The latter is of particular import to Burdett: "The curb is often the first barrier. A lack of curb cuts is what often keeps people at home."

This must also include better access to reliable public transport. Many people do not enjoy the same dense, compact, and connected cities as Maya. Fewer than half of households have access to a car; thus public buses, trams, and trains are a vital link in the accessible transport chain. But once again, many male planners see transportation through the lens of a "traditional" nine-to-five commuting pattern. This means higher levels of service during peak hours. "Whose peak hour are we actually talking about, though?" asks Dr. Burdett. She argues that reducing service and routes during "off-peak" is not so much a response to lower ridership; rather, lower ridership is a direct result of that reduced service. "People don't use off-peak service because it's often infrequent, inconvenient, and indirect," she insists.

In her work on equity in Auckland, Dr. Burdett found that 95 percent of people living with a disability said they needed access to a car because the public transport schedule didn't align with their non-nine-to-five life. "More than most other groups, they are more likely to have part-time employment, working more shift-related jobs, and earning less on average, particularly disabled women," she identifies. "It's not that people who have low incomes or disabilities don't want to use public transport, it's that it doesn't meet their needs." Like Maya, they have lives that include childcare, errands, and other day-to-day tasks performed by able-bodied individuals. "Once they purchase a car, why would they go back to public transport?" she asks. This lack of ridership, paired with disabling environments that make travel uncomfortable for anyone outside a car, leads to one of the biggest challenges in creating more accessible streets: How do you design for something you can't see?

Measuring the Invisible Trips

When transport planners look at a network, they design for efficiencies based on the trips people do take. They examine where they live, where they travel, and how to make those journeys as cost and time effective as possible. However, no one is ever analyzing or measuring the trips people don't take, which is particularly problematic for the disabled community. Think about the last time you were ill. When you're feeling a little sick, the last thing you want to do is take a 40-minute, meandering bus ride when a 10-minute taxi ride would be easier. If cities are designed like that—and we would argue most are—it puts people off traveling, or it makes those choices more expensive. For the disabled, Dr. Burdett insists that more often than not, the trip isn't made in the first place: "This affects people's well-being, because they wanted to do that trip, but due to either difficulties accessing suitable transport or financial hardship, they simply stay home." It happens to everyone, but some experience it more frequently than others.

It is particularly notable that these injustices affect people from a very young age. "Preschool is when we start seeing some of those inequities in cultures around the world," states Dr. Burdett. "Therefore, you have certain groups who are disadvantaged from the outset." When a young child can't access an early childhood center, for example, because it's not easy for their parents or caregiver to get them there, they are less likely to be at the learning level of a 5- or 6-year-old when they start school. As a result, they are less motivated to learn, leading to a raft of consequences that eventually impact their opportunities later in life. This includes the likelihood to secure a good job, and ultimately experience a high quality of life.

"Transport is the gate between our home life and everything else out there in the world. If it's not accessible, the consequences are reduced well-being and increased inequity," Dr. Burdett emphasizes. Choices in cities are biased toward those able to afford the luxury and time of driving around a place not designed for participation by everybody. Disabled people disproportionately experience mental health problems, which can be exacerbated by inaccessible environments. This increases the likelihood of disabled persons earning a lower income, which further reduces access, making it less likely that a given trip will happen. Dr. Aldred affirms this: "People with disabilities affecting their ability to travel make considerably fewer trips than those without. This can mean less access to education, employment, health services, social events, and leisure: all essential for social inclusion." For Dr. Burdett, it's about designing systems for humans, and all of their individual capabilities.

During the COVID-19 lockdown in New Zealand, which was one of the strictest in the world, Dr. Burdett conducted interviews of 300 people across the country, 90 of which were living with some form of physical disability. Twenty percent of disabled respondents stated that they had not left their home at all during the last week of lockdown, compared with less than 1 percent of nondisabled people. When she spoke to three of those disabled individuals, each expressed feelings of anxiety about the additional number of people on the footpaths. They worried about not being able to move easily out of the way to maintain physical distancing.

While this is an extreme case, it speaks to how many are simply not participating in society because it has been made uncomfortable or inaccessible to them. Imrie refers to this as the prisoner syndrome—where people are unable to independently interact with their environment, ultimately relying on others for their most basic needs. In his research, he found two out of five disabled people in the UK depend on someone's support to take trips out of their home for shopping, recreation, and other pursuits. "For people with disabilities, mobility, or often its absence, is a crucial context for reinforcing their subordinate and marginal status in society," he states. So how can planners and designers change this negative pattern?

Inclusive infrastructure means that 16 percent of trips made by physically impaired people in the Netherlands are pedal powered, often on an adapted bicycle. (Modacity)

Inclusion Breeds Inclusivity

"What I have learned is we need to do a lot more talking to people living in these experiences, to better understand their needs, wants, and requirements," Burdett asserts. She notes that in New Zealand, as well as elsewhere in the world, the traffic engineering profession is taught to provide for the motor vehicle, and not impede it at any cost. In her own neighborhood in Hamilton, a nearby roundabout was recently increased from one lane to two, due to a new housing development, making it impossible to cross by anyone not in a car. "This environment, in the middle of a residential area, is prohibitive to walk in, the barriers increased exponentially for people with a disability," she laments. Once again, the invisible trips and latent demand were ignored, leading to fewer choices. To Burdett, had they first engaged with people in the community, they would have been able to identify those with the greatest needs, where they lived, and how to better accommodate them. Increases in transport demand could have been accommodated with well-designed walking and cycling connections, rather than building an extra traffic lane.

This is the root of addressing and correcting traditional thinking to be more inclusionary. But Burdett is compassionate: "The range of human experience is so broad, and it isn't taught in schools. Until it is taught and measured, we need to rely on people with lived experience. Knowing their stories makes the argument against equitable design more difficult to have." And we simply must measure. When talking about inclusive access, there is no current model for data collection. To be successful, such policy needs to have some performance indicators to act as feedback loops; before and after studies can help determine whether what has been implemented has been effective and whether there has been increased participation. "An ideal end game is when we have a society where everyone who lives in a community participates equally as much as they want to," Dr. Burdett reiterates. "If we're not measuring the diversity of participation, then how do we really know?"

She also affirms that these principles apply equally to those with visual impairments. Quite often, as with the reasoning for maintaining car dominance, cycle tracks and shared spaces are seen as creating barriers for people whose sight is impaired. "The principles of universal access mean that they work for anyone, including those with visual impairments," Dr. Burdett emphasizes. "If we were to create a hierarchy for people with disabilities, then people who cannot see at all—and therefore can't drive—probably have the fewest choices and therefore the most need." Once again, she reiterates the best way to start the journey is by having good relationships with the local disability community, and to design solutions together.

There is even a place for technology in finding equitable solutions. For the visually impaired, apps connected to beacons in the city tell users their exact location, interior details, and streetscape elements. Recently, Burdett wrote a paper focused on counting mobility aids as an indicator of access, and then comparing those data to the proportion in the community. New developments in technology, combined with engagement and measurement, have real potential to help.

Underlying this potential for future success is the fact that, in order to create inclusive environments, we need to include everyone in the conversation. Burdett reflects on New Zealand's lockdown, and the celebration and optimism among activists with all the children outside biking and taking up the road because the cars had all but disappeared. Yet at the same time, a significant portion of disabled people didn't leave their homes. "When we can gather better information by engaging with the community regularly, then we'll get a better picture of what works," she says. "If we're not measuring, then we're just walking around blind ourselves."

Mix Where Possible, Separate Where Necessary

When it comes to building more inclusive and welcoming streets, what exactly sets the Netherlands apart? What explains the empowering and emancipating conditions that people with disabilities—people such as Maya—enjoy? The secret, many might be surprised to learn, lies not in a specific piece of legislation—such as the Americans with Disabilities Act—but with a single book. A product of decades of experimentation in Delft and other municipalities across the country, the CROW *Design Manual for Bicycle Traffic* is widely regarded as the best bikeway engineering guide in the world. But it is much more than that. Developed as a set of national standards, it is a book that simply assumes—much like space for driving—space for walking and cycling is a given, and must exist not as individual sections of road, but as a complete, cohesive network that takes the user anywhere they need to go.

Applying concepts that came out of the process of implementing the 1979 Delft Cycle Plan, the CROW manual dictates that any successful network must reflect five principles: cohesion, directness, (road and social) safety, attractiveness, and comfort. And while they are often viewed and applied through the lens of bicycle planning, they can also be extrapolated to the idea of universal access. Maximizing accessibility for the disabled is not a stated outcome but a by-product. By ensuring that these networks of active travel infrastructure can be accessed by the greatest number and diversity of participants, through design and proximity, they are inclusive and intuitive for everyone, even for those—like Maya—who don't even ride a bike. The directness imperative, for example, suggests that the length traveled on the network should never exceed the length of the direct path ("as the crow flies") by more than 20 percent, ensuring that travel distances remain relatively equal, especially for vulnerable modes.

While many cycling advocates assume that physical separation between bikes and cars is best practice in all conditions, the CROW manual actually takes a more nuanced approach. Its mantra can be summarized as follows: "Mix where possible, separate where necessary." Where feasible and appropriate, the speed and volume of motor vehicles should be reduced—to a maximum of 30 km/h (20 mph) and 2,500 cars per day, respectively—to allow for mixed traffic conditions. Only as a last resort, where traffic calming isn't possible—generally where cars exceed 50 km/h (40 mph)—then physical separation isn't just recommended, it is required.

Specific to those physically segregated cycle tracks, there is strict guidance on their width, to ensure a variety of speeds, masses, abilities, and comfort levels. And the importance of that additional width cannot be overstated. Whereas the *Urban Bikeway Design Guide* by the US-based National Association of City Transportation Officials requires a minimum one-way cycle track width of 150 centimeters (59 inches), the CROW manual requires a minimum width of 200 centimeters (79 inches) and strongly recommends a width of 225 centimeters (89 inches). That additional 50 to 80 centimeters may not seem like much, but it allows riding abreast and safe passing of slower users, and can often be the difference between a demanding challenge and an enjoyable experience. This kind of inclusive infrastructure is what draws the masses—of all abilities—onto their own streets.

When it comes to mixed traffic situations, the *fietsstraat* (bicycle street) is not exactly a new solution. Invented in Germany in the 1970s, and utilized in the Netherlands since the mid-1990s, they are fairly common on streets within residential areas, where cyclists already outnumber cars. They are characterized by a red pavement treatment, prominent branding (both on the street and on road signs), a reduction in the availability of parking, and traffic-calming measures that dissuade motor vehicle through traffic. These four features combine to make it abundantly clear that bikes are the main users of the street, and that drivers—as guests—should adjust their behavior to suit. People

The *fietstraat* (bicycle street) uses design features to make it clear that cyclists are the main users of the street, and drivers—as guests—should adjust their behavior to suit. (Modacity)

on *scootmobiels*, such as Maya—who regularly takes advantage of two parallel *fietsstraten* to commute to The Hague—are not explicitly mentioned in this treatment, but they certainly benefit from it.

Last but not least, the CROW manual contains specific requirements about the steepness of a gradient, ranging from 2 to 10 percent, depending on the height of the slope. This ensures that bridges, tunnels, and underpasses remain accessible to all users, reflecting the reality that they have different levels of fitness and skill and operate a variety of vehicle types. Like the abundant curb cuts, small ramps, and pedestrian bridges that double as cycling bridges (and therefore lack stairs) seen across every city in the Netherlands, these are the unexpected benefits of orienting your built environment around the bicycle. Cities that work for cycling also work for people using wheelchairs, strollers, rollators (rolling walkers), and many other types of mobility devices.

The Real Meaning of Accessible Streets

For Maya, those principles of cohesion, directness, and safety have played key roles in maintaining her freedom of movement. Despite living further away from the center of Delft, she enjoys no less access than her more able bodied peers. Originally from Israel, Maya knows firsthand what a less accessible city looks like. Although she had long moved from Tel Aviv prior to her illness taking effect, when she compares that environment to what she enjoys in the Netherlands, Maya knows she would not enjoy the same quality of life had she stayed in Israel when she was 18.

"My mother wants me to move back to Tel Aviv," Maya reveals, "but I would be giving up all of my freedom." She describes the city as a place where the car is king: a lack of curb cuts, narrow sidewalks, and high traffic volumes would leave her completely dependent on family and friends in order to get around. And on the occasions when she would insist on traveling alone, she's left choosing between navigating cramped, cluttered footpaths, or risking her safety by riding alongside cars on the busy roads. It's a compromise on her mobility that she's not willing to make: "I can go anywhere because there are bike lanes everywhere. It doesn't matter if there is a quiet street or busy street, I am always completely comfortable."

Attractiveness and comfort are probably the least revered of the five CROW principles for many planners and engineers, likely seen as the result of successfully achieving the first three. Regardless of ability, though, they are arguably the most important to the true success of a network. If people feel uncomfortable, or the infrastructure doesn't take them where they need or want to go, then it is a failure.

The extensive network and the ease and comfort of using it to get around Delft and the neighboring areas are why Maya not only loves living here, but why she is very reluctant to leave. That joy extends beyond getting to and from work, school, and the shop. "I am a nature lover; it is my relaxation," she reveals. "When I was really limited in my mobility, I was really bound to the city, and that was really a shame. I missed it so much." As a part of her rediscovery of activities to keep her moving following her relapse, Maya purchased a hand bike. "I love

The additional width of many Dutch cycle paths that allows riding abreast and safe passing of slower users draws the masses—of all abilities—onto their streets. (Modacity)

hand biking, but in Delft it is not so easy and a little stressful," she admits. Due to her illness, Maya struggles to maintain balance at times. So, within city limits, having to stop and start at intersections or negotiate busier areas with fellow cyclists is quite daunting.

Thankfully, because Delft is surrounded on all sides by pastures, forests, and grasslands, within 10 minutes, Maya is surrounded by nature. Additionally, in a country that has built thousands of kilometers of rural cycle routes, she doesn't have to sacrifice her comfort while doing it. People with disabilities often struggle to navigate uneven and rough gravel trails. The smooth, paved cycle paths throughout the country are vital to giving them equal access to nature. "I only discovered how close I was when I started using the *scootmobiel* and hand bike on the cycle routes in nature," Maya says. "I love the fact that there is planning for where people want to go." Through the combination of *scootmobiel*, hand bike, and services like RegioTaxi, there is no limit to how far Maya can travel on her own: "I'll go anywhere!"

In speaking to Maya, we have gained a new appreciation for what "accessible streets" really means. It's about much more than the technical design specifications, and about creating an environment in which, no matter whether you walk, cycle, or use a mobility aid, you feel safe, comfortable, and respected. "I feel so enabled because of the way that the environment treats me. If there's a car behind me, they don't honk or rev their engine—they know they have to wait. That nature of respect, it's very beautiful to see." Because the network is designed in a way that discourages car use, not only is it contributing to a quieter and cleaner living environment, it is also facilitating participation of groups that otherwise would be isolated: "My favorite part of getting around is bumping into people in the center. If I couldn't do that with my *scootmobiel*, I would feel very disconnected socially and very lonely."

Although not its intended application, the principles of the CROW manual and the networks that have been built over the last 50 years have ensured that anyone in the Netherlands, even those limited in their mobility like Maya, can maintain their independence and social connection to their community. Maya's experience shows that even as her physical abilities decrease due to the degenerative nature of multiple sclerosis, her ability to enjoy all aspects of life in Delft, the neighboring countryside, and the country as a whole will not diminish. Of all the things Maya shared with us, it was her parting words that helped us to really appreciate how this little cycling nation is actually so much more than just that: "You don't understand how truly wonderful the Netherlands is until you are disabled and you need to get somewhere!"

Chapter 8

The Prosperous City

The model American devotes more than 1,600 hours a year to his car. He sits in it while it goes and while it stands idling. He parks it and searches for it. He earns the money to put down on it and to meet the monthly installments. He works to pay for gasoline, tolls, insurance, taxes, and tickets. He spends four of his sixteen waking hours on the road or gathering his resources for it.
— Ivan Illich

When we made the difficult decision to sell our trusty Toyota Echo in 2010, giving up automobile ownership for good, we were quick to emphasize that we were—in fact—a "car-lite" family, and not a "car-free" one. While a fair number of the daily trips we made in and around our East Vancouver neighborhood could be covered on foot, bicycle, bus, or Skytrain, we were still regularly re-signed to car-sharing from one of the four private schemes available in the city. This was especially true whenever we strayed outside city limits for activities in the less transit rich parts of the region: a business meeting in industrial North Vancouver, a piano recital in suburban Burnaby, a trip on the ferry to the Sunshine Coast, or a day of hiking in remote Squamish. With an annual fee and a few swipes on an app, we could reserve one of a variety of motor vehicles—including compacts, SUVs, and minivans—and pay by the minute, hour, or day. While these fees certainly added up, we estimated we were reducing our monthly transportation budget by at least C$400. These savings, along with our subsidized rental housing, were the only things that allowed our young family to survive for so long in an increasingly unaffordable city.

It was during our first visit to Delft Gemeentehuis (Municipal

Hall), while registering as new residents, that we learned we had to make another difficult decision. When it comes to driver's licenses, the Netherlands has agreements in place with a few Canadian provinces, allowing newcomers to conveniently exchange theirs for a Dutch one. Sadly, British Columbia was not one of them. Despite both having licenses since the day we turned 16, we then had six months until ours expired; forcing us to go through the certification process from scratch. So we resolved to see how those first months went, and then make a decision from there.

The first step from there was to register each member of our family for an *OV-chipkaart*, the universal pass that provides access to every train, tram, bus, and shared bicycle in the country. These journeys are compiled, correlated, and invoiced on a monthly basis, the total of which is automatically withdrawn from our bank account a week later. Melissa, Chris, and Coralie opted to purchase the Dal Voordeel (Valley Advantage) season ticket, which for an extra €5 per month, entitled us to a 40 percent discount for train travel on weekends and outside peak hours. Etienne qualified for the Kids Vrij (Kids Free) program, which allows every child under the age of 12 to ride the intercity trains for free across the Netherlands, Belgium, and Germany.

Even without a driver's license, we soon found that the combination of cycling and public transport—fed by decades of investment in quality infrastructure, secure parking, and frequent service—made us more mobile than we've ever been. No matter where we travel in the country, we begin our journey with a short, five-minute roll to Delft Station, where we can pedal directly into the parking garage and store our bikes at no cost. From there, we tap our cards on turnstiles located at either end of the facility and hop down a flight of stairs to the platform. More often than not, there's no need to check the train schedule, as service is frequent enough that we seldom have to wait more than a few minutes for a train to Rotterdam, The Hague, or Amsterdam. Once we reach our destination station, sometimes having to connect trains in Rotterdam or The Hague, we can each borrow a blue-and-yellow *OV-fiets* (public transport bicycle) with another tap of our smart cards; knowing we will be charged €3.85 for each 24-hour period that passes until it is returned.

With the simple tap of their *OV-chipkaart*, Dutch train users can borrow a blue-and-yellow *OV-fiets* (public transport bicycle) for a 24-hour period for €3.85. (Modacity)

Of course, this multimodal option works well for destinations in urban areas, but we were pleasantly surprised at how accessible it also made suburban and rural areas. Whether visiting the tulip fields of Lisse, the beaches of Noordwijk, or a volleyball tournament in Zoetermeer, the combination of comprehensive rail coverage, complementary bus and tram networks, and safe cycle tracks made it easy to get virtually anywhere without a car. The limits of this range were tested when, in August 2020, our son registered for a summer camp in Westdorp—a village located 17 kilometers (10 miles) northwest of Emmen in the Province of Drenthe. After a two-and-a-half-hour train ride from Delft to Assen (with a connection in Rotterdam), we strapped his backpack to a shared bicycle, and pedaled for an hour or so through the beautiful countryside, passing dairy farms, cornfields, and evergreen forests.

Working for the Dutch Cycling Embassy also means that Chris

needs to attend various meetings, workshops, and study tours in every corner of the country. While most employers offer €0.19-per-kilometer reimbursement for car-based travel, he was more than happy to receive an NS-Business Card (an *OV-chipkaart* for employees) instead. Depending on the time of day, he has the option of cycling from our apartment to the main Delft Station or from the office to the secondary Delft Campus station. In addition to metropolitan areas, he has traveled by bike-train-bike to remote locations like a TV studio in the Port of Amsterdam, an industrial park south of Amersfoort, a regional office on the outskirts of Arnhem, a bicycle factory in the small town of Dieren, and a corporate campus next to a motorway in Breukelen.

This pattern became a daily part of Chris's routine when, in March 2020, the Dutch Cycling Embassy moved its headquarters to Utrecht, 70 kilometers (40 miles) east of Delft. In most regions, such an office relocation would cause a significant disruption. But in this instance, he simply joined the hundreds of thousands of bike-train commuters across the country, with no sweat. He had been in this boat before. His first job after moving to Vancouver in 2007 was for a small architectural firm in Abbotsford, a full 70 kilometers from our East Vancouver home. There, he had little choice but to make the daily slog along the TransCanada Highway in the aforementioned Toyota Echo, as public transport options into the Fraser Valley were nonexistent. Despite best efforts to carpool and telecommute, the stress of this drive was too much, and he soon took a pay cut to work within cycling distance (an income loss that was soon offset by the sale of our family car one year later).

Needless to say, the myriad mobility options we use on a daily basis have changed our lives, both personally and professionally. Like car sharing allowed us to become a car-lite family in 2010, the bike-train combination allowed us to become a car-free family a decade later, after our Canadian driver's licenses expired. In our first six months in the Netherlands, we had sat in a car just once: to return Etienne's bed to IKEA. Access to transport plays an integral role in our ability to continue living without a car, without sacrificing where we live, work, learn, and holiday. While this system can never be truly perfect, harnessing the synergy between bicycles and public transport may be the key to unlocking access to opportunity, including housing, education, employment, health care, shops, and essential services. Like it has for us, it could also be integral to freeing others from the economic burden of automobile dependency, leading to a more prosperous and equitable region.

The Role of Transport in Accessing Opportunity

Our experience is by no means universal with that of everyone in the Netherlands. But by sheer numbers, the marriage of cycling and public transport has been proven a success, with no less than half of all train trips beginning with a bicycle ride. This is important because it enlarges the station catchment area from a radius of 1 kilometer (0.6 mile)—a 20-minute walk—to 5 kilometers (3 miles). The latter is a reasonable distance for most, regardless of age or ability, to comfortably cycle, and covers diverse areas, from dense cores to outer suburban zones. This includes low-income neighborhoods, for whom the link to public transport, claims Jeroen Bastiaanssen—PhD candidate and researcher for the PBL Netherlands Environment Assessment Agency—is vital for social inclusion and access to employment.

Bastiaanssen spent several years working under Dr. Karen Lucas at the University of Leeds. Dr. Lucas is one of the world's leading experts on transport and social exclusion in the Global North and South. Together they collaborated on a report in 2019, *Inequalities in Mobility and Access in the UK Transport System*, which surveyed over 8,000 individuals to examine the relationship between transport and social exclusion. Their findings were nothing short of eye-opening. Two-thirds of the elderly (7.8 million people aged 60+) could not reach a hospital by public transport within 30 minutes. One-fifth of the working-age population (6.8 million people) could not reach a single large employment center by public transport within 45 minutes, compared to just 2.7 percent for those who traveled by cars. On average, car users could reach double the number of job centers as public transport users, in the same journey time. Nearly 6 percent of pupils aged 11 to 15 (168,720 people) could not access a secondary school by public transport within 30 minutes.

This publication was a follow-up to a seminal 2003 report by Lucas's Social Exclusion Unit, titled *Making the Connections*, which came to fairly similar conclusions: "Amongst low-educated job seekers, two in five specifically mentioned barriers related to transport impacting their ability to get to their place of employment," explains Bastiaanssen. "Additionally, one in four cited the cost of travel as a barrier." That's 25 percent of people already starting at a disadvantage, further affected by the cost of simply getting to a job. Inadequate transportation options, and a lack of a car—whether the prohibitive expense of purchasing a vehicle, or simply accessing a family vehicle—leaves large portions of the population behind, or doesn't even provide them with the opportunity to get ahead in the first place.

Bastiaanssen points to problematic land-use patterns as one of the inhibitors of this access. Chasing postwar modernist ideals, many countries, including the Netherlands, began to separate the functions of the city. Manufacturing jobs ideal for individuals with low income and low education declined in number and decentralized to the periphery. At the same time, low-income housing was built in other outlying areas of the city, due to larger plots of land available at reduced costs. The trouble is, public transport did not follow. This is where the disconnect begins.

"Often these individuals are traveling from outskirts neighborhoods, into the center where transport hubs are located, and then out to the periphery again," says Bastiaanssen. "That cost of traveling from a peripheral neighborhood to get to peripheral job centers and business parks is a greater burden for someone already living on limited means." Of course, the impact is not just economic. The time burden of using indirect routes, coupled with dependence on schedules that are often unreliable, leave few options. Those who can manage car ownership's financial toll do so not because they want to but because they are left with no choice.

"You see consistently throughout the years that roughly 10 to 15 percent of the unemployed in the UK mention they have to turn down jobs due to transport problems, specifically due to inadequate transport," Bastiaanssen suggests. Similar to Dr. Burdett's findings related to people with disabilities, buses that don't run on time, sudden

As seen in the suburbs west of Delft, secure parking at this stop feeds far more customers into the bus network, without impacting its capacity or reliability. (Modacity)

cancellations of service, and a tradition of reduced service during off-peak hours—paired with the location of employment opportunities and unconventional schedules—makes simply getting to one's job a sometimes-insurmountable challenge. "Low-income groups, low-educated, young people, even the elderly—basically everyone that doesn't have access to a private car—they tend to struggle more often to access these opportunities," explains Bastiaanssen.

In the United States, this problem of reduced opportunity was identified in a 1968 paper by John F. Kain, in which he coined the term *spatial mismatch*. The "white flight" of the 1950s saw most White people flee for the suburbs, leaving African Americans behind, and reinforcing segregation in regions of all sizes across the country, but especially larger urban centers. Paradoxical to the issues arising elsewhere from the peripheral housing and employment locations, Kain wanted to understand why Black people living in inner cities were still unemployed at higher rates when compared to lower-educated and lower-income White people.

"What he found," explains Bastiaanssen, "was an increase in spatial mismatch between where people lived and where employment and amenities had moved." As middle-income and White groups moved out of the centers, leading to increased car use and ownership, a lot of the employment and amenities followed: "What you see is that Black American groups were left behind in the city centers, unable to access those locations." Despite living more centrally, the available public transport options did not allow them to access the places they needed to in order to find and maintain a job, and this disproportionately affected people of color. It is a pattern seen in countless countries, as 70 to 80 percent of travel shifted from public transport to the private automobile. And in many of those places, it hasn't changed much since.

In a society where one's potential to thrive and prosper is entirely dependent on their ability to generate an income, transport or access to it is fundamental. So, it is no wonder that even in the poorest communities, car ownership continues to flourish. And although it solves the challenges of reaching employment, what is the true cost of car dependency, and how is it perpetuating social exclusion over time?

The True Cost of Car Ownership

Taking into account all costs—including depreciation, insurance, fuel, maintenance, financing, parking, and registration—the average American automobile costs its owner a whopping $12,544 a year (or $14,452 for an SUV). That's over half a million dollars across the course of someone's working life, per vehicle. With the average low-income household earning $20,000 to $50,000 annually (nearly 29 million households), that is not an insignificant sum of money. But despite the financial burden, within the bottom end of the labor market—those who typically don't use public transport because it doesn't meet their needs—car ownership is increasing. This growth is driving many families into debt, with Americans owing a total of $1.6 trillion on auto loans in 2018 (that's $4,875 for every man, woman, and child), a 75 percent increase since 2009. But it is debt that is almost required by the built environment: even in dense New York City, only 15 percent of jobs are accessible within an hour by transit, as opposed to 75 percent within an hour's drive.

According to a report from the Institute for Transportation and Development Policy (ITDP), "The High Cost of Transportation in the United States," US families own an average of 2.28 cars. Thirty-five percent of households are paying for three or more. As the ITDP states, "Personal vehicles accounted for the largest amount of transportation expenditures in 2017—a total of $1.1 trillion, almost 90 percent of total transportation expenditures." Meanwhile, there persists the narrative of the American dream: work hard and you will be able to escape poverty. "We've built cities that make this narrative impossible," it goes on to say. "For households making less than $20,000 per year, reliable cars are a pipe dream: a huge expense that they can't afford. Without adequate transit, they will remain stuck in place."

We often view the burden of car ownership as the expense of the vehicle itself, but in reality, it is the external costs—the ones not borne by the owner—that are often the most damaging, impacting millions of other people. There are, of course, the costs for infrastructure construction and maintenance (through the collection of municipal, state/provincial, and federal taxes), the health care costs associated with an increasingly sedentary society, and the environmental costs of a carbon- and diesel-burning society. Beyond these, however, are the hidden costs of a transport system designed to maximize automobile flow; costs that are downloaded onto households that don't have the means to purchase their own motor vehicle.

The average American spends roughly 13 percent of their household expenditure on transportation, but this proportion is not similar across income brackets. That same ITDP report points out that lower-income households typically pay a larger percentage of their budget on transportation. As people move up in income brackets, they tend to pay a smaller portion; however, the result is that those with the least means are burdened with the largest percentage of expenditure: "In 2016, in the US, the lowest-earning 20 percent of the population earned an average of $11,933, and spent an average of $3,497 (29 percent) on transportation costs."

Clearly, the poorest are hit the hardest by lack of investment in public transport. With acute emphasis on the continual movement of cars, and funds channeled to "solve" issues of congestion, the relatively small remaining portion of transportation budgets is left to be split between walking, cycling, and public transport, with the latter often losing out. Public transport systems are not cheap to operate, and lack of investment leads to the very thing causing this inequity in mobility: reduced schedules, cancellation of routes, and little capacity for transformative changes. "Personal vehicles are not cheap, and are not subsidized. But because American cities fail to provide people with alternative transportation options, people are forced to travel by personal vehicles," the ITDP states. Since 1956, highways alone have accounted for nearly 80 percent of all government spending in America's transport system, leaving precious little for other projects.

There is perhaps no better encapsulation of this problem than Toronto's Gardiner Expressway, an 18-kilometer (11-mile) freeway that has severed the city from Lake Ontario since it was built in 1955. In 2016, the municipal council voted to completely replace the crumbling arterial, including a 7-kilometer (4.3-mile) elevated section, at a cost of $2.2 billion. Between 2020 and 2030, that single piece of infrastructure will eat up 44 percent of the transport department's capital plan, despite moving just 7 percent of commuters (many of whom don't even reside or pay taxes in the city). Less costly, at-grade options were rejected by councilors after a staff report predicted that they might prolong peak driving times by two to three minutes.

The situation is no better in the United Kingdom. In the 2019 report Bastiaanssen coauthored with Dr. Lucas and others, they found that problems with affordability of daily automobility costs, or "car-related economic stress," were estimated to affect between 6.7 and 9 percent of households, corresponding to between 1.7 and 2.3 million households. In 2017, expenditure figures revealed that, for the first time, transportation expenses account for the single greatest proportion of weekly household budgets in the UK, narrowly surpassing housing.

"Low-income households are often found to lack sufficient resources to purchase and insure a private car, and to pay for fuel costs," the report reads. An investigation of the households vulnerable to fuel price increases in Yorkshire determined that fuel price increases are most likely to affect people in rural areas, where lack of public transport may force them to use a car to access key services. Unsurprisingly, in low-income households who do have access to an automobile, small changes in cost have potential to push them into economic stress. An analysis of the 2018 "Living Costs and Food Survey" found that in 2012, car-related economic stress was experienced in 9 percent of all UK households. For those in the lowest income bracket, this may be the case for as many as 67 percent of car-owning households.

The Intersection of Access and Economic Mobility

In a car-dependent society, the economic impact of car ownership and lack of public transport for low-income and historically disadvantaged communities is significant. In recent years, many researchers have focused on the qualitative effects on those who experience transport poverty. The outcomes negatively affect not just employment opportunities but also myriad public services necessary for a minimum level of well-being. Beyond access to hospitals and other social services, the economic mobility of individuals is impacted before some are even working age.

Bastiaanssen points to research in the UK that shows young people choose not to attend certain schools or universities because they are too far away or too expensive to reach by public transport. That access to education, be it in primary, secondary, or postsecondary institutions, has repercussions down the road, potentially limiting employment opportunities for these young people after graduation. Even if their concession for choice of educational institution doesn't adversely affect their career options, being able to actually travel to their job continues to be a challenge. Even if they try their utmost to escape a pattern of low income and education, their economic mobility is stunted simply by living in an area with inadequate transport options.

In the book *Building Equitable Cities: How to Drive Economic Mobility and Regional Growth*, authors Janis Bowdler, Henry Cisneros, and Jeffrey Lubell define *economic mobility* as the ability of an individual to move up the economic ladder. They argue that it is in the self-interest of cities to support and enable economic mobility because if their citizens thrive, so will the city. But more importantly, when everyone has the potential to thrive, cities become more prosperous and equitable.

"The ability of individuals to realize their economic potential should not be determined by the color of their skin or the location where they were born or the resources available to their families," the authors argue. But economic mobility and equity do not occur on their own. They must be planned, translated into policies, and then adopted. "For this to occur, we need a process that works systematically and incrementally to turn the vision of an equitable city into a reality," they claim.

Of course, policy is rarely driven by qualitative research. Policy makers rely on quantitative evidence to predict whether a change will positively or negatively impact those affected. Bastiaanssen recognized this, using his PhD to compare labor force surveys from the United Kingdom and the Netherlands, using an econometric model to estimate the impact of accessing jobs using a car, public transport, bicycle, and a combination thereof. His research examined travel during both peak and off-peak hours, on every neighborhood level, looking at how many job opportunities could be reached, and whether that was related to someone's probability of employment.

"What you see is that especially in groups that are overrepresented in unemployment—the lower educated, lower income, younger people—they typically are more sensitive to changes in their level of job accessibility," says Bastiaanssen. "This establishes a causal relationship between someone's job accessibility and their probability of employment, especially among the low-skilled, low-income, and young people." In effect, if an individual's ability to both find work and travel to it are directly linked to the reliability and accessibility of public transport, and if that system breaks down, they will experience significant, highly negative impacts, most significantly, a loss of income, or even the loss of their job. Their economic mobility is completely reliant on a physical mobility network that is historically unreliable.

Investment in improving public transport and making it more reliable, and thus more equitable, is essential. "If we increase the modal accessibility levels by 10 percent, then we expect the employment rate to

The advantages of providing secure cycling infrastructure and parking can be seen in many locations, such as the tram lines that extend north to The Hague. (Modacity)

go up roughly 1 percent for lower income groups," reveals Bastiaanssen. He suggests that a lack of economic mobility is caused by a lack of sectoral collaboration: "Transport, education, health, and housing sectors aren't working together to ensure accessibility, and no one takes responsibility." Furthermore, he notes that when transport sectors focus so much on car travel and "solving" the "problem" of congestion, they direct resources at demographic groups that already have relatively high access to opportunity.

A constant struggle hinges on the reality that individuals with lower education or incomes—just as with women and those with disabilities—don't work within the bounds of the traditional nine-to-five model. They are more likely to perform shift or part-time work, requiring mobility options that are available early in the morning, midday, or later in the evening. But with consistent cuts to public transport, largely at the expense of building and maintaining roads, services during these presumed "low ridership" periods are drastically reduced. Instead of regular, frequent service, they rely on schedules possibly operating on half-hour to one-hour headways, often taking less direct routes. If someone lives in a peripheral neighborhood and has to travel through the center and then out to a peripheral employment center, relying on such a limited system is an unrealistic expectation.

The issue is only compounded for women. Limited schedules combined with indirect options provide little to no ability to trip-chain. Take, for example, the experience of a low-income single mother: to arrive at her place of employment on time, she must get her child(ren) to daycare before going to work. Assuming she works within more traditional working hours, she still has to begin this journey early enough to get to the other end of the city on time, a trip that may take at least an hour. To arrive by 9:00 a.m., she will likely have to begin that journey between 7:00 and 7:30 a.m., just before many peak services begin. At the end of the day, she is again under constraint, reversing the journey to reach childcare before they close, typically around 5:30 p.m., again, with the trip commencing outside of peak service, and likely followed with other errands, including shopping for food and supplies for her family. The time costs alone for this commute are unsustainable, and the commute is successful only if the system is operating at normal efficiencies. Change just one element—like a canceled bus or train— and the whole system breaks down. Adjust her situation to part-time or off-hours shift work, and it becomes impossible; leaving her with no choice but to purchase a car and manage that financial burden.

When investments in public transport are made to improve the system, including MaaS (Mobility as a Service) based models like car- and bike-sharing, they are often located largely in city centers. While these can be viewed as a net positive, they are focused on places that need them the least. "The whole public transport system is based on the needs of higher educated groups, concentrated to the centers, and to locations where they need to go," Bastiaanssen says. "As soon as you need to get outside of those centers it is much more difficult, certainly if it's outside those corridors." This significantly limits social and economic mobility.

"This is why I am generally skeptical about MaaS initiatives and transport innovations," states Bastiaanssen, "because I don't see it changing people's travel patterns or behavior, or at least the way they think. If you look at surveys where they ask people if they may be interested in these initiatives, you see the early adopters are always young people and high-educated groups; typically the groups that already make use of public transport or bikes and are in need of the least help."

As with finding solutions for gender, disability, and age equity, access to transport for those with lower education and income levels is not addressed because it is underrepresented in studies. The Canadian census, for example, only asks about journey to work data, as do countless other countries. National surveys rarely ask questions about the opportunities that participants are potentially missing, and the impact access to transport has on them. Why aren't they traveling? Are they experiencing difficulties? What are the consequences (missed employment, health care appointments) of not making that journey? Unless the trips not made are measured to better understand how many people are affected and how often, including those that might be unemployed due to lack of transportation, the economic mobility of people without access to physical mobility will remain stunted.

In her article "Transportation Emerges as Crucial to Escaping Poverty," author Mikayla Bouchard refers to a 2015 Harvard study that named commuting time as the single strongest factor in the odds of escaping poverty. "The longer an average commute in a given county, the worse the chances of low-income families there moving up the ladder." But if we never provide the opportunity to make that commute in the first place, those chances evaporate. Creating equitable cities where everyone has the chance for upward economic mobility is inextricably linked to mobility, or more specifically, access to reliable mobility that exists beyond a pay-to-play system. Only when they step away from a car-dominant model to one that focuses on diverse, collective transport options that work for anyone—regardless of their income, education, ability, gender, or race—can cities truly become equitable.

Combining Bikes and Trains to Replace the Car

Boasting over 3,200 kilometers (2,000 miles) of track connecting 410 different stations, the Nederlandse Spoorwegen (Dutch Railways) is an outstanding example of what's possible with a more balanced approach to transportation investments. When regions don't allow the private automobile to dictate and dominate their budgets and priorities, it frees up all kinds of funding to improve the speed, frequency, and coverage of their public transport. For Delft residents, this means—taking connections into account—202 daily trains to The Hague, 182 to Rotterdam, 168 to Utrecht, and 150 to Amsterdam. And that's before the third and fourth tracks go into operation in 2024. With 81 percent of the country's population living within 7.5 kilometers (5 miles) of a station, the national railway operates like a national metro system. Much like investments in road infrastructure induce more traffic, these investments in rail infrastructure induce more and more passengers (at last count, 1.3 million nationally per day; 32,000 of whom arrive or depart at Delft Station), with many of these hubs forced to enlarge and renew to increase capacity.

Delft Station is one such recently upgraded facility, having been built to replace a 130-year-old building, and opened in 2015 as part of the project to twin and bury the train tracks underneath Phoenixstraat. Designed by local architects Mecanoo, the striking, teal-and-gray glass structure integrates the station hall with the city's municipal offices, including a new bus loop, tram hub, and bicycle parking facility. Fed by a pair of segregated, sloped cycle tracks on either side of the station, the parking facility includes space for 5,000 bicycles in two-tiered racks, with digital counters indicating the number of free spaces in each row. Within days of opening, it became abundantly clear that that wasn't nearly enough. Officials scrambled to build a secondary facility that opened in 2018, with space for another 3,700 bikes. Even that proved to be insufficient, with a third facility under way, which—when complete in 2021—will total over 10,000 spaces. In the meantime, those first two facilities operate at 98 percent capacity, and the need for bike storage spills onto the street, with temporary two-tiered racks placed at several points around the station.

Keeping in mind that—for the same time and effort—someone can cycle five times farther than they can walk, these larger catchment areas actually play a critical role in feeding more customers into the public transport system. And they may—at least to a certain extent—tamp the demand for housing in and around train stations. Assuming

With 81 percent of the Dutch population living within 7.5 kilometers (5 miles) of a train station, the national railway operates more like a national metro system. (Modacity)

a fairly even population distribution, one can extrapolate that roughly 10,000 residents live within a 15-minute walk of Delft Station, whereas all 100,000 are within a 15-minute bike ride (not to mention even more in the surrounding municipalities of Den Hoorn, Schipluiden, Delfgauw, and Zweth). This was a particularly intriguing perspective coming from Vancouver, where skyrocketing real estate prices were all the more expensive within walking distance of a Skytrain station. This huge appetite was visible in the city skyline, with dozens of glass towers clustered around each transport hub. We couldn't help but think the bike-train combination might flatten that curve, and disperse demand a little more evenly, providing exponentially more people with access to the Skytrain network.

Delft's regional connectivity becomes all the more impressive when you consider that Delft Campus—a secondary station on the southern edge of TU Delft (Delft University of Technology)—is undergoing

The demand for secure bicycle parking has far exceeded supply at Delft Station. When a third facility is complete, there will be a total of 10,800 spaces available. (Modacity)

a similar upgrade. When complete in 2024, the rail capacity will be doubled, and walking and cycling connections improved, with several hundred covered parking spaces provided for patrons. Notably, a solar panel roof will provide all necessary electricity, making it the first energy-neutral station in the country. Not only will this enhanced service offer additional flexibility and frequency for Delft residents near the center, providing a viable alternative to the car, it will do the same for many of the lower-income neighborhoods on the periphery of the city.

The advantages of providing secure cycling infrastructure and storage extend beyond the national rail system. It can be seen in many, less-prominent locations, such as the bus stops in nearby De Hoorn, and the tram lines that extend north to The Hague and Leidschendam. Since customers are widely discouraged to bring their bicycles on board—as it affects the capacity, reliability, and scalability of the system—reliable bike parking is provided for the first mile, and a shared bicycle for the last. To that end, there are over 400 *OV-fiets* available to rent at Delft Station, along with a service desk that offers repairs to personal bikes. These investments in bicycle parking, rentals, and service make perfect economic sense for public transport agencies, as they increase ridership and revenue. Rather than treating the bicycle as a competitor, it is seen as an ally—one that connects passengers to their origin and destination; a critical component of the seamless door-to-door journey.

Breaking Down Barriers to Opportunity

These kinds of collective investments in a frequent and flexible public transport system—to maximize its convenience and coverage—are precisely what governments must do to lighten the financial burden of car ownership and break down the all-too-real barriers experienced by those lowest on the socioeconomic ladder. But far too often, untold billions are spent widening roads to benefit those who already enjoy the greatest proximity and privilege, while mass transit that would benefit those who need it the most is chronically ignored and underfunded. By doubling, and then tripling down on car dependence, and mandating costly automobile ownership, regions are quite literally holding themselves back, preventing entire swaths of the population from fulfilling their true economic potential. The tremendous cost of car dependency continues to blow a giant hole in our governmental and household budgets, and everyone ends up the poorer for it.

As the Dutch demonstrate, providing a diversity of mobility options—especially the option to leave the car at home—is what ultimately creates a more affordable and prosperous society. It has the added bonus of actually solving congestion. But without comfortable walking and cycling conditions, and a reliable bus and train service, the automobile will remain the first choice for many families. In that scenario, everyone loses, especially the drivers. This is evidenced by the fact that the Netherlands is regularly found to have some of the lowest levels of urban traffic congestion in the world. It should go without saying that taking vehicles off the road is far more functional and cost-effective than continuing down the vicious circle of building more roads; a circle to which American cities such as Los Angeles, Denver, and Houston can attest; all of whom have wasted billions widening highways, only to have travel times return to previous levels within a few months.

For many households, shrinking the portion of their transportation budget would go a long way to help them achieve financial stability, and even lift some out of poverty. For our family, it has given us the luxury of working a little bit less. When the two of us were offered the option of a four-day work week at the start of our employment with Mobycon and the Dutch Cycling Embassy—a growing practice among employers in the Netherlands—we weren't sure whether the prorated salary would be enough to comfortably cover rent and other monthly expenses. But we hesitantly gave it a try, and within a few weeks, we really came to cherish that additional day off. Fridays are now reserved for quality, kid-free "us time," exploring the cafés and museums of Delft. It's our one day of the week to reconnect with each other and with our city, an unexpected by-product of our decision to go car-free.

Then, when our 12-month probationary contracts were made permanent in the spring of 2020, we immediately approached a *make-laar* (real estate agent) about purchasing a property in the Delft area. Having watched houses in our East Vancouver neighborhood go from C\$300,000 to C\$3 million in just over a decade, we had long given up on the idea of homeownership. But in this case, we were no longer limited by the walking distance to shops, services, and public transport; nor were we forced to compete with the high demand for such proximity. With the extended range provided by pedal power, we could suddenly open up our search to entirely new parts of the city: Haanteje to the north, Tanthof to the south, Voordijkshoorn to the east, and Vrijenban to the west. An equitable region is one that provides residents with the same access to opportunity, regardless of their postal code. With a national rail network and national cycling network at our disposal, we know we can live virtually anywhere in the Randstad, without compromising on our lifestyle and our employment opportunities. And for us, that's a great place to be.

Chapter 9

The Resilient City

Americans have a thousand choices for breakfast cereal, and one for mobility.
    — James Wilson

W e can recall the exact moment the COVID-19 crisis became all too real for the residents of Delft. It was the afternoon of Friday, March 13, 2020, and having spent the morning rolling through the polders of Midden-Delfland, Chris stopped at our local Albert Heijn for some lunch supplies. Melissa had left the night before for a business trip to the UK and could sense a looming tension among her fellow travelers. She encouraged Chris to purchase some extra supplies "just in case," as walking into a few shops herself, she noted that people were starting to stock up.

What greeted him was an alarming scene from a postapocalyptic movie, as entire families—who had removed their kids from school—were emptying the shelves of bread, milk, flour, and toilet paper. After watching the deadly news spread from China to the Middle East to Europe, cases had been confirmed at the local hospital, reportedly TU Delft (Delft University of Technology) students who had returned from spring break in Northern Italy. Something had swiftly changed in the minds of our neighbors.

That evening, Prime Minister Mark Rutte went on television to advise the normally level-headed Dutch to avoid *hamsteren* (hoarding) essential items, announcing an "intelligent lockdown" that would close workplaces, schools, and restaurants for the foreseeable future. Melissa returned two days later following an eerily quiet trip on the *Eurostar*—a stark difference from the full train we had taken the prior summer. We were all grateful that she wouldn't be stranded as airlines began canceling flights. Nonetheless, arriving safely in Delft was a relief.

In 48 short hours, every study visit, social engagement, and business trip we had planned for spring and summer were completely wiped from the calendar. All of the children's extracurricular activities immediately paused, and like many other families, we hunkered down in our apartment, trying to make the most of a terrible situation. We then watched in horror as COVID-19 swiftly took its toll, destroying hundreds of thousands of lives and millions of livelihoods across the planet.

The following weeks created a distinct shift in the feel of Delft's streets. With trips outside of the home drastically diminished, the quiet corridors we had already enjoyed became almost silent. But the silence was soon replaced with more birdsong than we had ever heard. A blackbird had taken refuge in a large evergreen next to our terrace, sharing its song with us each morning as we enjoyed breakfast, before starting our work- and school-days from our kitchen table, and each evening as we used our outdoor space as reprieve from having been trapped at our computers all day.

We also started taking walks in our neighborhood and city center each evening, when the number of people out running errands or traveling to essential jobs lessened. With virtually no car traffic, we, like many others, took to walking in the middle of the street to ensure that we could maintain safe physical distance. But despite a general feeling of fear and uncertainty, the social trust and connection we witnessed and experienced only grew during lockdown. Everyone we passed would smile and say a kind, "*Goedemiddag*" (good afternoon), and we saw our neighbors check in on each other, making sure they were happy and healthy, and helping each other however they could. Even the so-called Cats of Delft seemed to be behaving in a more friendly manner, happily jaunting over for attention—although that could have had more to do with them reclaiming their streets with those pesky humans locked away.

What was difficult was seeing our families in Canada living a more "locked down" existence. Our retired parents tried to go for short walks when they could, and our siblings would take our young nieces out when possible to maintain space, struggling to keep them off play structures and at a distance from passersby. For most trips, however, they were largely dependent on driving to amenities, meaning they were spending more time indoors and alone. Although the streets in their suburban cities had become quieter, the freedom we felt here in Delft was certainly lacking—an irony of course when we think of how wide many of those roadways are.

For our family, most of our day-to-day needs could be met within comfortable walking or cycling distance of our home, on broad cycle tracks or traffic-calmed streets with plenty of physical space for safe passing. In the rare instance we had to stray farther to Rotterdam or The Hague, we could avoid the train—and save that precious seat for someone who needed it. Cycling the entire 15 kilometers (9 miles) to an appointment in Rotterdam wasn't a typical practice for us, but it was manageable under the circumstances. And we weren't the anomaly in this decision.

We had experienced comparable disruptions in the past, albeit on a smaller scale, and were amazed at how the multimodal transport networks of the Netherlands complemented and supported each other during times of duress. When we hosted a housewarming party in late 2019, we learned mere days before that track maintenance meant no intercity trains were stopping in Delft that weekend. We sat and waited for many of our guests—who were coming from elsewhere in the country—to cancel. Instead, we were pleasantly surprised when nearly every guest eventually arrived at our front door, some pedaling from Den Haag Centraal on an *OV-fiets*, some catching the Rotterdam Metro to nearby Pijnacker, and others taking the bus-tram combination from Leiden. And yes, a couple even drove their cars.

Delft is also very much a work in progress, a city that has been undergoing a great deal of growth and transformation, especially around the redeveloped Delft Station. With this construction has come the inevitable disturbance from streets, tunnels, and bridges that are closed, sometimes for days at a time. But despite the blockages and detours,

Not everyone will choose to cycle long distances, but having the option allowed us to avoid the train—and save a precious seat for someone who needed it. (Modacity)

people on foot and bicycle keep moving, seldom delayed for more than a minute. We saw this firsthand when, in November 2019, the main cycling route to TU Delft was closed for an entire week. For most means of travel, shutting down a corridor that moves 21,000 people a day would cause chaos and gridlock. But in this case, traffic kept flowing to adjacent streets as if nothing had happened.

By prioritizing pedestrians and cyclists over a fragile car-based system, Delft has positioned itself to deal with the challenges of a twenty-first century city below sea level: including fuel shortages, rising temperatures, and extreme weather. And as it turns out, it was also well placed to deal with a global pandemic. In the months that followed those first days of lockdown, the biggest change to our daily existence was that we were no longer traveling to work or school each day, and had reduced our trips to the grocery store. Without knowing or planning it, we landed in a place where the built environment

Eighty percent of Dutch urban roads are calmed to 30 km/h (20 mph) or less, with car access restricted, creating plenty of space for physically distant active travel. (Modacity)

helped mitigate the physical and emotional impacts of a worldwide catastrophe, a place resilient enough against external stresses that it helped residents take care of themselves and each other under the most difficult of circumstances.

Applying "Resilience Thinking" to Our Cities

Resiliency has become a bit of a buzzword in recent years, especially in urban planning circles, but unlike *sustainability*, it does not enjoy a unified definition. This often makes it open to interpretation, depending on the eye of the beholder; something Dr. Judith (Y. T.) Wang— an associate professor in resilient transportation at the University of Leeds—is working tirelessly to correct. The term was originally coined by Canadian ecologist C. S. Holling in 1973 as "a measure of the persistence of systems and their ability to absorb change and disturbance and still maintain the same relationships between populations or state variables." This is the concept with which most people are familiar, but two decades later, Brian H. Walker developed a second definition: "the amount of change a system can undergo before it crosses a threshold and flips to an alternate stability regime of that system." As Wang maintains, these are understood as the two present-day faces of resilience: the former as "engineering resilience," the latter as "ecological resilience."

"For engineers, 'engineering resilience' is easy to understand," Wang explains. "By instinct, they want to design something that lasts forever, what we consider a 'fail-safe' design." To achieve that, they focus on three things: *efficiency*, *constancy*, and *predictability*. But an ecologist sees this issue from a different angle: "'Ecological resilience' focuses on *persistence*, *change*, and *unpredictability*," she describes. In other words, since change and disturbances are inevitable, it is also okay if the system flips to an alternate stability domain, that is, a "fail-safe" design.

Regrettably, engineers often overlook the latter's importance, fixated instead on absorbing disturbance and returning to "normal" as soon as possible. But from an ecological perspective, if the disruption proves too much, a "new normal" can—and in many cases, should—be created. "Resilience thinking is to consider both engineering and ecological resilience in dealing with disturbances to any system, including the physical components and users of the system," Wang summarizes.

To explain this important contrast to her first-year civil engineering students, Wang asks them to imagine a hypothetical bridge connecting two halves of an imaginary city. In the design and construction of this bridge, a team of engineers and planners would collaborate, bringing their varied perspectives and skills to the process. "The civil engineer would look at the structural design of the bridge, in order to maximize its strength and beauty," posits Wang. "The traffic engineers would look at the layout and traffic management of the bridge, in order to maximize the possible flow at an acceptable speed." Naturally, both the civil engineers and the traffic engineers would take care to ensure the "engineering resilience" of the bridge.

But what about the planners? "The transport planner might think about what modes are allowed on the bridge," suggests Wang. "They would also think about what happens if the bridge is unavailable or destroyed by flood. Can people still travel to work or school? Is there an alternative route?" The urban planner, meanwhile, takes this exercise a step further, wondering what happens if residents on each side of the bridge have to remain there for an extended period of time (or even forever), whether life would still be manageable in their half of the city? Essentially, is each side of the bridge designed to be functional and livable, in and of itself? "I think the transport and urban planners are natural thinkers of 'ecological resilience,'" says Wang.

To that end, Wang suggests it is much more helpful—and accurate—to view the built environment through an ecological lens, rather than an engineering one. "It is well known in the planning world that the form of a city, its urban environment and the way we live are the results of the choices made under different policies," she says. People decide how to travel day by day; in the longer term, they choose where to live and where to work, based mostly on what they think might be best for their family, especially the next generation. Despite vast improvements in technology and speed over the decades, the average work commute has remained remarkably consistent at about an hour. "Our choices are linked dynamically, and the system evolves with our decisions," claims Wang. "The result is a complex system within which we all self-select into our most comfortable environment and way to live."

This evolution is most recently apparent following the approach in various cities to enabling physically distant transportation post-lockdown. During this period, some North American cities—including Oakland, Austin, and Vancouver—recognized they had a responsibility to help maintain the physical and mental health of their residents, who were otherwise trapped indoors for days at a time. So, they quickly opened up miles of "Slow Streets," barricaded corridors where through traffic was prohibited, and locals could get outside and walk, jog, roll, or socialize in a responsible and physically distant manner. As the end of the lockdown period approached, many European cities—including Berlin, Lisbon, and Paris—announced entire networks of "pop-up" cycling infrastructure, not one or two routes, but dozens that would connect as many origins and destinations as possible, in an effort to keep their streets moving postpandemic. Seeing the lack of options for residents, the system adapted to meet their needs, even if temporarily.

This enlargement of the walking and cycling realm emerged not from a sense of opportunity but from one of necessity. In London, physical distancing measures meant their public transport network could only operate at one-fifth of its usual 10 million passengers per day (not to mention many who were hesitant to share close quarters with others). If 8 million people suddenly jumped into a car each day—on top of existing traffic—the streets would soon collapse under their weight, with huge impacts on congestion, noise and air pollution, and delivery times. To make up for this lost capacity, there would need to be a fivefold increase in miles walked, and a tenfold increase in miles biked. These two scenarios were quantified for the Italian government by Amsterdam-based Decisio Onderzoek: doing nothing would cause an increase in car use whose externalities could cost its cities up to €20 billion per year, while intervening and replacing these trips with active travel could save them an extra €20 billion per year. The question was no longer whether cities could afford to invest in walking and cycling. It was whether they could afford not to.

Comprehensive Resilience in Transportation

If we want to accurately measure the resilience of this evolving ecosystem, we must look at not only the urban form but also its inhabitants. "But how do we represent the resilience of people?" Wang queries. The physical and mental health of residents is one important attribute we can measure. The social cohesion and trust of their community is another. Communities that rate better on these qualities would obviously fare better when the unexpected strikes. "In my view, the resilience of a city and its inhabitants is inter-linked, and they need to be improved together in a systematic manner," explains Wang. Building infrastructure to support walking and cycling can be useful only if residents are willing and fit enough to give those activities a try. "Urban planning and transport planning can transform our city only if the inhabitants are willing to transform themselves as well," she concludes.

Having grown up on the abundant buses and trains of Hong Kong (a region where 88 percent of journeys are made by public transport and 7 percent by private car), Dr. Wang never even considered learning how to drive. But when she landed her first lecturing position at the University of Auckland (a region where 4 percent of journeys are made by public transport and 83 percent by private car), she gained new insights into the difference between a sprawling, car-dependent city and a dense, compact one: "Which is more resilient? I think the answer is clear. In Hong Kong, I developed my skills to be an independent traveler at an early age." Never having to worry about finding time for physical activity, Wang could fill up her schedule with a variety of activities any time of the day and any day of the week. In Auckland, when she worked in the Central Business District, she put on weight from not getting enough physical activity, especially walking. "Most importantly, I lost my freedom and independence!" Wang laments. "My schedule and possible activities were dependent on whether I would have a driver to take me and bring me back."

Much like Maya's experience living with a disability, Wang's mobility, or rather her freedom of mobility, was dependent on a system not built to meet her needs or abilities. There is a constant struggle in a car-dominant system: the network is built on the assumption that everyone can and will drive, forgetting that at any one time, as much as half the population *cannot* drive. This includes children, the elderly, people living with disabilities, people without the means to buy a car, or those who simply *choose* not to own or drive a car. Especially during lockdown, this means the network leaves those people stranded or completely dependent on others, which, even in ideal scenarios, only works if the system doesn't break down.

In the following years, Wang went on to define "comprehensive resilience in transportation" as the quality that leads to *recovery, reliability*, and *sustainability*. By its very nature, a car-dependent network lacks all three of these qualities. Any shock to this brittle system—a spike in fuel costs or a natural disaster—makes recovery very difficult, if not impossible. This was made abundantly clear during the 2008 oil price spike, when prices went from US$50 per barrel to US$140 overnight; triggering a global financial crash as mortgage and car loans could no longer be paid. When Hurricane Harvey hit Houston in 2017, the flooding destroyed as many as a million cars, leaving many families scrambling for alternatives: rental cars, ride-hailing services, public transport, and yes, even bicycles. An estimated 100,000 did not have flood insurance, meaning they had to pay for a replacement out of pocket.

Secondly, travel times within a car-dominated transport network are notably unreliable and heavily dependent on the presence of congestion, roadworks, weather (like rain, snow, and ice), and collisions. This can be witnessed in the vast number of suburban commuters who depart for work in the wee hours of the morning, in an effort to "beat" traffic and inject some reliability into their routine.

Of course, no conversation about reliability would be complete without a mention of safety, an area in which car travel is notoriously unreliable. The World Health Organization estimates that a staggering 1.35 million people are killed and 50 million injured by automobiles each year (disproportionately affecting lower-income residents and people of color). In the European Union, 150,000 people are permanently disabled by crashes annually. If any other transport industry possessed this safety record—whether airline, maritime, or railway—it would be shut down immediately. These injuries and deaths are not inevitable, but rather the product of car-first design that prioritizes their speed and movement over all other considerations. Streets can be engineered in a more forgiving manner, and drivers encouraged to behave more appropriately, evidenced in the differing fatality rates between the Netherlands and the United States. The Dutch experience 3.4 annual deaths per 100,000 inhabitants, the U.S. 10.6; a rate that—if successfully transferred across the Atlantic—would save 20,000 American lives per year.

Finally, car travel is clearly unsustainable. Motor vehicles are a major contributor to air pollution, producing half of carbon monoxide and nitrogen oxides, and a quarter of hydrocarbons emitted into the atmosphere. They are a significant contributor to climate change, accounting for one-fifth of all emissions in the United States—around 24 pounds (11 kilograms) of carbon dioxide for every gallon (3.8 liters) of fossil fuels burned. But these problems don't begin and end at the fuel source. Tires and brake pads emit 550,000 metric tonnes (606,271 US tons) of microplastics (particles smaller than 0.01 millimeters or 0.0004 inches) each year, with nearly half ending up in the ocean. Over 80,000 metric tonnes (88,185 US tons) end up on ice- and snow-covered areas, increasing melting as they absorb heat. This problem is likely to get worse before it gets better, as electric cars are heavier than internal combustion engine cars, which means more stress on the vehicle's tires and brakes.

We seem to be entering uncharted territory, and some regions will be harder hit than others. "The frequency and intensity of extreme weather events is increasing, and we are already suffering from an irreversible use of limited natural resources," Wang says. She points to the correlation between fuel consumption and the built form. Atlanta, for example, needs 2,960 liters (782 gallons) of gasoline per person per year for its urban system to work. Barcelona needs just 242 liters (64 gallons). This ability to adapt becomes all the more important when you consider that our world is constantly evolving. "Change is the one thing that is permanent in life. Climate change, for instance, is only one ongoing change that we are dealing with," Wang suggests. Just as change is constant, so is the need for sustainability. "If we flip to a different stability regime, that must also be sustainable," she emphasizes.

Transforming the City and Its People

For a few short weeks, the COVID-19 lockdown transformed the way Dr. Wang and her neighbors experienced the streets in a small town in North Yorkshire: "Many people around the world were suddenly able to see their beautiful cities under the blue sky again! There was no noise, pollution, or hazard from traffic. People claimed the road space back, and started walking in the middle of the road without fear." She also recalls speaking to some of her neighbors for the very first time, who—when they learned she worked in transportation—admitted that they liked their street without all of the traffic. Dr. Wang insists that this is another key ingredient in meaningful change: "Coronavirus is an opportunity to transform not only the city, but also the mindset of the people." But she's quick to clarify that it doesn't need to be revolutionary: "The point of 'resilience thinking' is not to overhaul the entire system, but to introduce multiple stable regimes. Not to transform into something else, but to become more transformable, and find somewhere in between as a 'new normal.'"

What should this "new normal" look like? According to Wang, maintaining *diversity* and *transformability* is a key to survival of any ecosystem: "We know that diversity is the key for ecological resilience, so this is the time to focus on what we have overlooked for years." This means building *diverse*, flexible, and reliable options into our transportation networks, and breaking up the monopoly enjoyed by the private automobile in most cities. And the months and years after a crisis are a critical time in which to establish this new regime. "Before the pandemic, we had one normal equilibrium. Based on the fundamental principles of 'resilience thinking,' we need the capability to easily flip to a different stable equilibrium," Wang explains. "To enable us to do that we need diversity not only in our system but also in our minds."

In the first six months of the COVID-19 crisis, over 2,300 kilometers (1,430 miles) and €1 billion of cycling measures were announced across Europe, which were tracked on the website of the European Cyclists' Federation, and ranked by city and country. To the surprise of some, at the bottom of the list was the great cycling nation of the Netherlands. But this makes perfect sense when you realize that the Dutch have spent the better part of 50 years building tens of thousands of kilometers of segregated cycle tracks and traffic-calmed streets, and in many ways, were perfectly placed to weather this crisis. Rather than scramble to provide alternatives for passengers avoiding the trams, buses, and trains, municipal governments understood that (e-)cycling could replace a good portion of those trips, because the door-to-door networks of infrastructure already existed. In fact, the only significant changes they made were to disable "beg buttons" and adjust the timing of traffic lights, to optimize intersections for pedestrians and cyclists, whose exposure levels exceeded those of people sitting in cars, especially when pedestrians and cyclists were bunching up at the street corners. The existing systems were simply adapted to enable a new way of moving.

To understand why Dutch cities didn't experience the same "mad dash" to reallocate street space, historians point to six weeks in the autumn of 1973, when their country experienced a crisis eerily similar to the one in 2020. At that time, the Netherlands was one of five countries targeted by an OPEC oil embargo, resulting in an abrupt gasoline shortage, and compelling its three million motorists to reevaluate their relationship with their cars. A dramatic spike in fuel prices forced many to reacquaint themselves with their bicycles—the sales of which doubled—producing a collective desire for safer streets. This shift was reinforced by the national government's Car-Free Sunday policy. Suddenly, for one day a week, cities went totally silent, and their thoroughfares were returned to the public realm. It was an instant in history when many residents realized they could no longer take certain things for granted, while simultaneously discovering the vast amount of space in their cities reserved for automobiles. Their reaction to this crisis was one based on ecological resilience, and a new stable equilibrium was sought by the politicians and the public. Decades later, about one-third of trips are made by active means, one-third by public transport, and one-third by private automobile.

The United States, meanwhile, which was subject to the same embargo in 1973, chose a very different postcrisis direction, one centered on engineering resilience. For the first time, an external force was imposed on their gasoline supply chain, leading to widespread panic, with people locking themselves down, queuing for hours, and hoarding supplies. However, their reaction to adversity was to double down on car dependency, in an attempt to return to "normal" as quickly and painlessly as possible. Decades later, about 5 percent of trips are made by active means, 5 percent by public transport, and a shocking 90 percent by private automobile.

Even in the midst of a climate emergency, many cities continue to look at resiliency from the engineering perspective, and resist the change needed to weather this biggest of crises, which will lead to floods, fires, cyclones, hurricanes, and typhoons. By building up their resistance to these events with a windshield worldview, and stubbornly adding road capacity and redundant routes, they may be creating higher car dependency and making things worse by decreasing their ability to pursue comprehensive resilience. Therefore, *transformability* becomes the key. "In ecology, resilience is not just about the capability of the system to get back to what is considered as normal after disruption, but also about the capability to be able to transform when it becomes impossible to return to normal," Wang explains, reiterating that it will take a change in both policy and mindset. "If our system cannot get back to normal after a disturbance such as the coronavirus crisis, then this is our opportunity to transform ourselves and the city together," she insists.

One such opportunity consists of enabling increased walking and cycling among children, which has no negative effect but which has proven difficult due to our long-term "normal" equilibrium induced by a car-dependent transport network. It is one of the many means necessary to help cities achieve comprehensive resilience in transportation. "With less people driving their kids to school, we can have a better environment with fewer vehicle emissions, which will also help slow down climate change," suggests Wang, pointing out that the time it takes to walk or pedal to school is almost entirely predictable: "Travel time reliability is perfect, and parents and pupils will form a stronger community." In the process, children will also learn to be more independent and thus become happier and more resilient as they grow up. "What we need is the transformation of our system and our mentality to embrace the diversity of choices, as well as multiple equilibria of how we live our lives," Wang concludes.

Mitigating the Effects of Climate Change

The diversification of our urban and intercity mobility networks is obviously critical in achieving comprehensive transportation resilience, as well as reducing their related pollution and carbon emissions. But as cities like Delft have discovered, providing these various alternatives also creates opportunities to mitigate the detrimental effects of climate change. Over the years, they have reduced the amount of asphalt dedicated to the movement and storage of motor vehicles, which demand a colossal amount of space: 20 square meters (215 square feet) when parked, and 140 square meters (1,500 square feet) when moving at 50 km/h (30 mph). This removal of pavement leads to the expansion of

In 2009, this signalized intersection at Delflandplein was converted into a roundabout; a paved area of about 5,575 square meters (60,000 square feet) was cut roughly in half. (Modacity)

green space along these corridors, which is valuable in dealing with rising temperatures and extreme weather, such as flooding.

With "road diets" such as the one undertaken at Delflandplein in 2009, not only were the adjacent roads reduced from four lanes to two—creating room for trees, grass, and shrubs—but the transformation of the signalized intersection into a roundabout also led to the creation of a vast area of greenery. A paved area of about 5,575 square meters (60,000 square feet) was cut roughly in half, with the perimeter and center of the traffic circle filled with flowering sedum, wild grasses, and perennial plants. In addition, the redevelopment at Delft Station includes new park space specifically designed to retain stormwater during the rainy season.

The amount of concrete and bitumen in cities presents a variety of challenges, not the least of which is the ability to manage stormwater runoff and associated waterway pollution. In the United States, paved surfaces cover 111,369 square kilometers (43,000 square miles), an area the size of Ohio. According to the Center for Watershed Protection,

65 percent of this impervious cover consists of streets, parking lots, and driveways; what they refer to as "habitat for cars." These surfaces collect all kinds of pollutants and particulates, and then release them directly into rivers and oceans. In urban areas, 30 to 50 percent of rainfall runs right into waterways, drastically raising the risk and severity of flooding. "Hundred-year floods" are becoming increasingly common, fed by a changing climate and extreme weather events. By creating more landscaping, including green roofs, this rainfall can be absorbed by the plants and soil, and retained for a longer period of time, while the community of micro-organisms acts to breakdown pollutants.

Then there is the *urban heat island effect*, which is also fed by the vast—and often growing—amount of concrete and bitumen surfaces in cities. With little vegetation and moisture to capture heat and cool the landscape, these surfaces simply absorb solar energy during the daytime, and then recirculate it at night. According to a 2009 American Meteorological Society study, nighttime temperatures can be as much as 10 degrees Celsius (14 degrees Fahrenheit) hotter in New York City than in rural areas 100 kilometers (60 miles) away. With rising global temperatures and the concentration of carbon dioxide in the atmosphere, this temperature disparity between urban and rural areas is only going to increase. The roofs of buildings are obviously one contributor, and greening or whitening them could help. But as with stormwater management, a more fruitful strategy would be the greening of streets.

In fact, the growth of greenery in the city could not only help improve biodiversity, control stormwater runoff, and reduce the urban heat island effect, the photosynthesis process of plants and trees could actually remove airborne carbon from the atmosphere and sequester it in leaves, wood, and soil. An estimated 50 square meters (538 square feet) of tree cover can sequester 4.5 to 11 kilograms (10 to 24 pounds) of carbon. According to the GreenBuilt Alliance, there is a range of landscape-based mitigation strategies that, if employed at mass scale, can help reduce greenhouse gas emissions by 50 to 85 percent by the year 2050.

In Delft, as with other cities like Rotterdam and Amsterdam, there are even places where the transportation network runs on top of green space. The practice of "greening" tram tracks has been around for

"Greening" tram tracks, as on Delft's Martinus Nijhofflaan, can decrease surface run-off, aid with the urban heat island effect, and reduce air and noise
pollution. (Modacity)

several decades, and offers myriad ecological and economic benefits
to the built environment. Greening 2 kilometers (1.2 miles) of double
track—with sedum or grass—creates a green space of 10,000 square
meters (107,639 square feet), or one-and-a-half football fields. This
green space can offset the negative impact on natural water balance
by reducing surface run-off, increasing water retention, and preventing
overload of the sewage system during heavy rainfall. The evapotranspi-
ration of plant material also aids with the urban heat island effect, decreasing air humidity and increasing the absorption of solar radiation.
It can also help reduce the amount of local pollutants on a given street,
absorbing both noise pollution and fine particulate matter in the air.

The electrification of the transport network is seen by many as the
singular solution to these sustainability issues, ignoring many of the
inefficiencies built into a car-based system. It would, for example, be
a much easier lift if the vast majority of the required energy—renew-
able or otherwise—wasn't wasted on 2,000 kilograms (4,400 pounds)
of dead weight, a machine that weighs 30 times more than the human

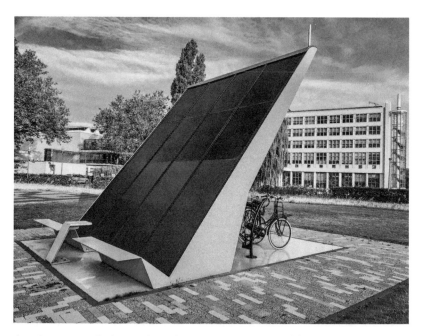

A solar-powered electric bicycle charging station at TU Delft. A mobility solution that checks all boxes for resilience, it is recoverable, reliable, and sustainable. (Modacity)

it's propelling. This is even more striking when you consider the Tesla Cybertruck, expected to weigh in at a whopping 4,500 kilograms (9,920 pounds), no less than 72 times more than the (likely often) single occupant it is carrying. There simply isn't enough cobalt, lithium, neodymium, or copper in the world to provide batteries—let alone the electricity supply—for all of these heavy cars and trucks.

Alternately, the pedal-assist electric bicycle has proven to be a popular alternative to the private automobile—at least where the infrastructure, parking, and subsidies exist. In 2019, TU Delft even went as far as building a demonstration project on campus: a solar array capable of charging up to four electric bikes. Small wonder the Dutch government was promoting them as a viable alternative to public transport during the COVID-19 crisis, for journeys up to 20 kilometers (12 miles) in length. This is a mobility solution that checks all three boxes for comprehensive transportation resilience: it is recoverable, reliable, and most definitely sustainable.

Crisis as a Turning Point

The COVID-19 crisis didn't just create a cycling revolution. It also led to a dining one, as cities such as London, Boston, New York, and Montréal quickly reclaimed many of their streets, curbside spaces, and parking lots to create "outdoor dining districts" to support their bars, cafés, and restaurants postlockdown. Business owners who may have fought against the removal of parking outside their front door were suddenly in support, as they saw value in repurposing it for something more valuable (and vibrant). As with the pop-up cycling measures seen elsewhere in the world, we experienced very little change in Delft. On June 1, the national government announced restaurants could open again as long as the 1.5 meter (5 feet) social distancing *maatregelen* (measures) were maintained. With most of Delft's communal patio space created long ago when the streets and squares of the city center were stripped of cars, all restaurateurs needed to do was bump their tables a little farther apart, and claim the additional 25 percent of terrace space afforded to them by the municipality.

For Americans, the OPEC oil crisis was a missed opportunity, but one they hopefully won't repeat, as discussion of a Green New Deal emerges to aid the COVID-19 recovery. Critically, this stimulus can't just switch the fuel source for all of the cars in the country, but must also include recoverable, reliable, and sustainable alternatives. This is underscored by a 2012 report by the American Association of State Highway and Transportation Officials, which quantifies the average number of full-time jobs created by infrastructure type. Amazingly, greenways, sidewalks, and bicycle facilities top the list at 17.0 jobs per million dollars spent, whereas pavement widening and highway construction create just 12.5 jobs per million dollars.

Active travel's impressive return on investment—in terms of job creation, public health, pollution mitigation, and reduced congestion—is abundantly clear to business leaders in Sydney, Australia, a region where 70 percent of residents indicate they would like to cycle more often. Unsafe conditions mean that barely 1 percent do, leading to a staggering two million car trips under 2 kilometers (1.2 miles) each day. There, a post–COVID-19 economic stimulus is being pushed by a coalition to accelerate their 5,000-kilometer (3,100-mile) cycle network plan—originally scheduled to be finished in 2056—from a 36-year timeline to just 3 years.

More walking and cycling can also improve a city's *economic resilience*, as they can be used to stimulate the local economy. In an age where one can get virtually everything delivered to their door—including groceries, restaurant meals, household items, and entertainment—small businesses can really only compete by drawing people out of their homes. This is accomplished not by providing a convenient place to drive and park their automobile but by offering serene, social, stimulating experiences that are impossible to resist. Furthermore, most of the money families spend on their car—such as fuel, insurance, and the cost of the vehicle itself—leaves their community. According to a 2012 report by the National Building Museum in Washington, DC, if a US city reduced its rate of ownership by 15,000 cars, an additional $127,275,000 would remain in its local economy. In a post-COVID world, the main challenge becomes bringing people back onto public transport systems that may have reduced their operating budgets, service levels, and attractiveness over the car as a piece of personal protective equipment.

In the first few weeks of lockdown, Delft city center became a proverbial ghost town, with only essential shops staying open. Luxuries like locally roasted, sustainably sourced beans from our favorite coffee shop owned by a lovely young couple, or dining at one of the many restaurants seemed impossible. But once again, the dense network of cycling infrastructure became part of a solution. Within days of the closures, websites started popping up with local businesses teaming together to provide customers in and around Delft the opportunity to continue buying from their favorite retailers, and have the goods delivered to their door by bicycle. We soon started receiving packages—coffee from our favorite coffee company, groceries from the nearby green grocers, flour ground at the nearby windmill, and even beer from one of our craft breweries. We even did the same for our family in

Canada, ensuring that birthdays and holidays were still meaningful during a pandemic. These options for hyperlocal, sustainable delivery meant these entrepreneurs—many of whom were our neighbors—could compete with the Amazons and Uber Eats of the world, and a situation that might have forced them to close their shutters allowed them to thrive.

The question that now remains is whether the COVID-19 pandemic and the ongoing climate crisis will be enough for car-dependent regions to pivot and create a "new normal." But their reaction to the coronavirus lockdown, and the unique conditions experienced by people across the planet, has allowed for some optimism. In the book *Resilient Cities: Overcoming Fossil Fuel Dependence*, Peter Newman and colleagues write, "Resilience is built on hope, which gives us confidence and strength. Hope is not blind of the possibility of everything getting worse, but it is a choice we can make when faced with challenges. Hope brings health to our souls and bodies." Now that millions around the world have experienced "low stress" streets firsthand, with far fewer cars and much more social interaction, we truly hope they hold onto those feelings, and transform that single moment into a movement for meaningful change.

Chapter 10

The Aging City

We should raise our sights for a moment. What could a street—a street on which our children are brought up, adults live, and the elderly spend their last days; where all people can move naturally with dignity and freedom under their own power; and where we all are able to celebrate our humanity together—what could such a street be like?

— Bruce Appleyard

I n 2020, we both turned 40, reaching that point when people inevitably think about what they've done with their lives, and where they go from there. Although some might say the move to the Netherlands was a sign of an impending midlife crisis, we would argue it was the natural progression of a search for a place that suited a lifestyle we'd been pursuing since walking along the water in Bilbao, Spain, on our honeymoon and thinking, "This pace of life is pretty amazing." As it was, the closest we got to a true midlife crisis was a pair of sleek *omafietsen* (granny bikes)—Melissa's in Ferrari Red—so we could roll around Delft in style.

That isn't to say a period of reflection hasn't crept in. Our journey from suburban Ontario to the west coast of Canada, and finally to the serene streets of Delft has been one of self-discovery, jammed with many events, including marriage, children, and career changes. Looking ahead, we now have a clearer picture of how we want to spend the next 40 years. We loved our lives in Vancouver, but it was always understood that it was a place in which we likely couldn't grow old. We wanted to be able to slow down, and live in a calming environment, but we didn't want to sacrifice the walkability, bikeability, and overall connectedness we enjoyed in our East Vancouver home. Now that we've landed in Delft, we think we may have found just the place to "settle down" and grow old together.

After spending a year and a half observing our older neighbors maintain active lives, getting on their bikes nearly every day, and interacting with each other and the younger residents in our area, we admired how attached they seemed to Delft. This was first exemplified in the communal effort to rescue Melissa from her lock-out situation; when we were first introduced to Peter de Kat, our 67-year-old *buurman* (neighbor) who also happened to be the handyman at our son's school. Peter had lived on our street since the day he was born, making us curious about what had kept him there all these years.

Born in number 12, he had moved to number 13 as a young man, and eventually purchased number 15, where he has lived for nearly four decades. "I have never left this street in my whole life," Peter laughs. Neither, as it turns out, has his family. Chris, age 70, his brother who lives directly across from us, has also remained throughout the years. With two other brothers, ages 73 and 81, living in house number 3 and just around the corner, respectively, the street is a bit of a family affair. Only their sister, age 78, moved away. "It's nice living here," he says. "My neighbors have also lived here a very long time. It shows that we like living here. We are very satisfied, the feeling is good, and the atmosphere is good."

Clearly, living on this street is about more than the house Peter lives in. When he purchased his current home for €30,000 after his former neighbor asked if he knew anyone who would be interested in buying it, he started a renovation with help from his friends and neighbors. A bachelor himself, he created room for lodgers, sharing his home with others and meeting many new people in the process. It is explicit very quickly that Peter is a social person. Whenever we run into him in the city center or having just returned from the store, he is sure to ask us how we are, how our Dutch is coming along—"Hoe gaat het met je Nederlands?"—quick chats that make us feel welcome as outsiders.

It should come as no surprise that following military service in his early 20s, Peter spent the next 40 years teaching Delft's next generations. "I chose it because I found it easy," he admits. Others, including us, would disagree—having the patience to teach is a skill not possessed by many—but his stories reveal that through this work, he built relationships with many families in the community. He recounts one student who was really struggling when he joined Peter's class. Teaching Groep 8 (the last year of primary school), Peter met this child when he was 12, and after several challenging weeks, and even Peter's threatening to remove him from the class, they found common ground, with the young boy finding his way. Unfortunately, the attention he received from Peter was not continued in high school, and the boy returned to old habits, but Peter had made such a strong impression that at a particularly low point, the boy showed up on Peter's doorstep on Christmas Eve and—as it turned out—his 16th birthday. "I knew he must be sad to have nowhere else to go than to his old teacher's house, so I welcomed him in." And that is exactly who Peter is, and why, when Melissa was locked out, our neighbor Marieke knew just whom to ask for help.

Peter is the first to admit he constantly needs to be active, so even after retiring from teaching, he remains involved with the school system. We're fortunate to benefit from his involvement since that school is Etienne's, where Peter practices his hobbies of photography and filmmaking, capturing the *werkweek* excursion the students take in their final year, as well as filming their end-of-year musical. "I'm doing what I want to do," he says. "It takes time but I'm proud of it." His passion is evident, so much so that other schools want his help!

Peter is a fixture both in our neighborhood and also in the city at large. Having taught at several schools across Delft, he often bumps into former students or their parents when walking or cycling. "It was always quite funny; every time I came to a new school, there were always parents who said, 'I know you,'" he recounts. "Every once in a while, they would be parents who I had taught when they were kids!"

Our neighbor Peter has lived on our street since he was born there in 1953. He has never owned a car; Delft offers all he needs within a short distance. (Modacity)

Having that intergenerational connection is something Peter has come to appreciate, being the social person that he is. "I remember that I used to be shy when I bumped into students when I first started teaching and would hear, 'Hi, *Meester* Peter,'" he admits, "but now I like it."

Having never owned a car, Peter has always traveled around Delft by foot or bike, and does so to this day. Being so visible when he's out of the house, it makes those opportunities for informal chats plentiful. Peter admits, though, that he doesn't need to know someone to start talking to them. "I'm very open-minded and love talking to people, even complete strangers in the elevator," he laughs. "Most people like it. I don't always know them, but they seem to like it." That openness is something we've come to expect from many of the Dutch people we encounter; enter a doctor's office, pass someone on a trail, or bike past a group in the rain, and they will say a friendly "Goedemorgen" or make a comment on the weather: "Slecht weer, hé?" Whether it's a cultural trait, or due to the more human way of moving through the city, it seems to be the way Peter lives—and enjoys—his life. "I'm doing what I want to do," he says. "I stay very active, it's very important to me."

Peter's desire to remain active is not just for his physical health, but also his mental health. His brother Chris—our window neighbor whom we often see petting his cat Tiger—is sadly in the early stages of dementia. "It's good that he lives nearby," Peter explains, "because I can watch over him and take care of him." Peter helps schedule his doctor's appointments and checks in on him every day to make sure he is okay. Luckily, though, Chris can still enjoy some independence, with routine and familiarity being so important. Four times a day he walks to the nearby grocery store, passing familiar places and faces along the way. Having that routine helps him feel connected to his community. We often pass Chris while we're out on our own walks, saying hello as we pass. Often there is a moment of unrecognition, but even if he doesn't remember us, the kind interaction always brings a smile to his face, and we're grateful to be a happy moment in his day.

"Because of my brother's health, I know it's very important to stay active, not just physically but also mentally," Peter states. Using his decades of experience as a teacher, Peter has been tutoring students in mathematics for three years. "It started with one student whose mother knew me and asked for my help," he explains. "Then she had a friend whose son also needed help." He reveals that he now tutors several students at a time in math and language, keeping him on his toes mentally, and also connecting him with the next generation, passing on his knowledge. He explains that he's not just teaching them; they're also teaching him. With new theories and methods, Peter often has to Google new concepts or watch videos to help his students. "For me it's a way to be also active in your mind."

Perhaps we were just lucky to find ourselves on this particular street, among these particular people, but we think it's more than that. Generations of building cities that work at a human level have created countless clusters like this, where people feel so comfortable and "at home" that they are now living out their senior years in the same places they grew up. Having come from a city where it was rare to see older residents so active in the community, it is remarkable to now watch, every day, countless retired neighbors like Peter out chatting with each other, or taking care of the street they live on. Something about the way the streets act as places keeps people living comfortably into old age. As Peter tells us, "I am attached to the environment here, and that I know where everything is, and I don't need anything else." What a way to live, and something we wish for our own parents in the years to come. But what do we need to do, on a global scale, to help our elderly achieve such an enjoyable way of life, and afford them the dignity of being able to age in place?

Organizing Space to Age in Place

Peter, his siblings, and a number of our neighbors are practicing what many planners strive for in cities around the world: to allow the elderly the ability to age in place. Its basic definition is as follows: People are enabled to age in their own home or in their own neighborhood for as long as possible. It is something many in their midlife look for; a place where they can retire and grow old comfortably. The truth is, however, for those living in car-dependent neighborhoods, especially expansive suburbs, staying in their home well into old age is an unrealistic idea. It all comes down to how the space is organized.

Dr. Bettina van Hoven is an associate professor of geography at the University of Groningen's Urban and Regional Studies Institute. She has spent a number of years exploring how cities can better support the elderly segment of their populations, including bringing a group of students from the Netherlands to Vancouver each summer to study how a North American city incorporates aging-in-place principles. Through her research, she finds that the definition of aging in place can be framed in both a positive and a negative way.

"The aim is to organize the neighborhood in such a way that it will enable people to live independently for as long as possible," she explains. In Dutch cities, something that has received an increasing amount of attention is the idea of having the things important to one's daily life, particularly for older adults, within a walking distance radius, about 500 meters (1,640 feet) of their home. "That is what research has shown that people can manage in one way or another with or without a mobility aid," Van Hoven explains. "And within that radius is the place that they live, the shops they visit, public transport, health services, and some recreational facilities, among other things." But without support from the built environment, once they inevitably lose the ability to drive, aging in place involves being trapped at home; leading to social isolation, physical inactivity, and loss of autonomy.

Much like the travel patterns of mothers and people with disabilities, many of the journeys taken by seniors include some form of trip-chaining, connecting multiple segments, albeit short ones, at times that are convenient to their daily routine. Facilitating trips such as these is at the core of La Ville du Quart D'Heure (the 15-Minute City), an idea developed by Professor Carlos Moreno of the Sorbonne, and popularized in the mayoral campaign of Anne Hidalgo in Paris. Picked up by the C40 Mayors as a part of the Green and Just recovery plan, La Ville du Quart D'Heure is defined as a city in which all of your daily needs are located within 15 minutes on foot or bike. For the elderly, this is particularly important, as with older age also comes reduced stamina. What for someone in their mid-30s may seem like a quick and easy jaunt to the store could take their grandparent two to three times longer.

Van Hoven insists that within these short journeys, places for rest are vital. "We need to think not just about the facilities at points A and B, but also those along the way to make the entire experience more comfortable." This includes resting places with shelter, because weather shouldn't necessarily be a limitation to someone's ability to make scheduled and unscheduled trips. The WHO Age-Friendly Cities and Communities checklist of essential features identifies the provision of benches as a key urban design resource for age-friendly cities. "It's interesting that often from a planner's perspective places can work because they are people-friendly or age-friendly, but what is often missing are the little details of how people use spaces." Think of the application of a dropped curb: someone may think they have a good sidewalk and are meeting the needs of the disabled, the elderly, mothers with strollers, and so on. But if that drop is not on the route they actually need to use, it's very inconvenient. For someone with limited mobility or stamina, this potentially increases their travel distance, and could lead to them not making the journey at all.

In cities built for and around automobiles, it means that sidewalks may not exist in many places. Additionally, how spaces are organized and connected may not work for the elderly. In the United States, for example, pedestrian crossings are designed so that 85 percent of users can get through in time, explicitly excluding others from participation. With these considerations, Van Hoven identifies that often, even if someone can travel by bus, the journey to that bus stop and then to their final destination can be impossible. "If you considered many of the big box shopping centers in more suburban contexts, they are not designed for travel on foot," she says. "You have to get in your car and drive the 100 meters to the other shopping centers because it's not safe enough to walk there."

In the book *Age-Friendly Cities and Communities: A Global Perspective*, the authors go further, noting on page 173 that the quality of public transport, including the location of stops and routes, is critical in the mobility of the elderly: "Many older people view public transport such as buses as unreliable, time-inefficient, and disability unfriendly or non-existent in their local areas. Inadequate public transport as well as damaged or poor-quality footpaths inhibit community engagement especially in socioeconomically disadvantaged neighborhoods."

Street Activity as Urban Life

Beyond the organization of the built environment, Van Hoven argues that just as important as enabling aging in place is the social support provided by the neighborhood. "This is not just one's family," she explains. "It's also the neighbors, the people living on their street, even the people working in the shops." This can be an unpredictable variable, easily impacted by busy lives and changing priorities. However, while the elderly fare better with regular, continuous social patterns in their daily activities, through her research, Van Hoven found that this concept of predictability doesn't have to be linked to specific people. "When you look at social isolation, the things we found that were also important were things that we sometimes don't notice. For older adults we spoke to, the life on the streets and the sense of predictability and regularity within that scope is really important."

She provides an example. Someone takes a short trip to the shop to get milk or bread, something they do every other day. For them, it's

For older adults, it is critical to create public spaces that enable "place ballet," which permits them to create daily rhythms and recognize faces on the street. (Modacity)

important to have faces they recognize on the street, to create daily rhythms, or what is called "place ballet." "People have these geographies and intersect in different nodes," she explains. "In certain important places, it's not that they know all these people, but rather that they see them, recognize them and say hi or are greeted." These kinds of "Hi–Hi" contacts are really important because they help people feel like they belong, like they are part of the life on the street. Her research showed that older adults find value in small talk while they are shopping. The simple act of an employee asking them about the purchase they made, or not getting impatient or creating pressure during a transaction helps them feel more welcome.

In *Age-Friendly Cities and Communities*, it is noted on page 85 that many older people who need care want to remain independently mobile for as long as possible. This includes doing their own shopping and maintaining their own social contacts: "Mobility restrictions were viewed as threats to self-determination and health, resulting in isolation and loneliness." Having these opportunities and possibilities in their neighborhood is even more important for those who depend on their locality. "In the Netherlands, 60 percent of the most important relationships in older people's networks are located in the neighborhood. Older people with fewer economic resources and a decreased activities of daily living capacity seem to be more dependent on their neighborhood as a source of social contact."

Furthermore, Van Hoven reveals it is not only about direct contact with familiar faces on the street, but also indirect contact. Even if they can just observe it from their window, they feel less isolated: "It's important not only that older adults can go somewhere, but also that if they stay at home, the place encourages the community at large to be outside and interact, giving that older adult something to look at and making them feel that they are part of the life on the street." What may not seem significant to how the average adult may think about social networks in daily life, for someone entering the fourth age of life (80+) it's risky to make significant social connections due to the risk of injury, health issues, or death. "These small interactions keep them connected and keep their daily lives more regulated." Older adults need more regularity in their lives, so smaller things become a lot more important: "For an older adult, the street activity is, for them, also urban life."

It is therefore understandable that aging in place is often associated with "attachment to place" as an important dimension of later life. The longer older people have lived in an area, the more likely they have developed stronger emotional feelings and an affective bond with their neighborhood. Experiencing the day-to-day life of their neighbors helps, even through the window, limiting feelings of isolation and loneliness, and without the risk attached to forging new bonds later in life. The challenge is that the average daily rhythms—or time geographies—differ between generations. Think of students who run on different schedules from adults, and again from the elderly. The existence of street life has changed, especially as more women work outside the home. Van Hoven suggests that having non-age-segregated community activities can support better intergenerational interactions.

It doesn't have to be complicated. "Life on the street and predictability and continuity at least in some shops help create those reliable and diverse connections," says Van Hoven. She points to some Dutch grocery stores that provide places to sit and have a free coffee, increasing the potential for social interaction and chats with staff and other regulars in the shop. Some supermarkets even offer training to their employees to practice awareness and patience, offer help when needed, and even recognize signs of isolation or health issues in older customers: "That is really important: to identify what are the places people use in their everyday lives and train people to become part of the social network."

"We're not talking about becoming best friends, we're talking about people in the network that can have a meaningful role in someone's well-being," Van Hoven clarifies. She argues that the seemingly benign act of a postal worker knocking on someone's door to check on them can have a huge impact on reducing feelings of isolation, and can even catch signs of decreased health: "These are all small steps that you must be able to implement more widely in cities to ensure that people have some kind of interpersonal contact."

The Age-Friendly City as the People-Friendly City

Due to the car-dependent nature of many cities, as long as people can still drive, they can still participate in society. As soon as they're no longer able to operate a motor vehicle, if there is nothing within walking distance, they are stuck. Small wonder that, according to the American Automobile Association, "Seniors are outliving their ability to drive safely by an average of seven to ten years." Often experiencing visual impairments and delayed reaction times, the elderly tend to adjust their driving patterns to less congested areas and daylight hours. This results in a dangerous situation not just for the user but everyone around them, as research from the RAND Corporation suggests drivers over 65 are 16 percent likelier to cause a crash.

The lost autonomy that comes with a loss of driving isn't limited to North America, either. Chris recalls when his grandfather—who lived in a midsized city in Warwickshire, England—had his driver's license revoked, causing him to go into a minor state of depression. After a lifetime of independent mobility, he was now completely reliant on his adult children to drive him and his wife to appointments, or wait for a bus that ran on an hourly basis (if it showed up at all). This is the unfortunate experience of many aging adults, and it can result in their being institutionalized in care homes earlier than they would like, simply because it is difficult or impossible for them to remain in their house and retain a normal daily rhythm.

Social inclusion—or exclusion—is heavily impacted by how urban space is planned and built. From seating opportunities, to nonslip surfaces, and lighting, welcoming environments can be created that encourage people of older ages to make the trips they need throughout the day. But only if they are reasonable in length for both their ability and their stamina. In the Netherlands, 30 percent of trips by people over 65 are pedal powered. The proliferation of e-bikes enables them to stay independently mobile for longer. While this holds myriad benefits for maintaining their physical and mental health, these trips are only viable if the streets are planned to allow for safe, comfortable cycling, no matter the person's age.

Van Hoven is quick to note that while she is a geographer and not a medical professional, it seems obvious that walking and cycling are good for physical health, "But how you define physical health includes affective physical and social well-being, and those also contribute to people feeling better." She suggests that when people feel better, they are more inclined to take these small outdoor excursions to the shops, for example. "However, if they have had a negative experience, either due to a negative interaction with the physical environment or the social environment, the next day they might not want to go out and walk, even if it's only 500 meters. I think those two dimensions are quite interconnected."

Although active travel is inherently good for seniors, there is also the risk of injury. Therefore, the quality of the space and how it is organized are vital. In Dutch cities, although streets often separate modes, they are designed in a way that takes into account the fundamental act of walking, based on the understanding that at any point in someone's journey, they will walk. The material selection, surface treatments, and curb heights combine to create inclusivity. In terms of cycling, Van Hoven implores cities to think about where people's lives

From seating to forgiving curbs, welcoming environments can be created that encourage people of older ages to make the trips they need throughout the day. (Modacity)

take place: "In this context, we don't necessarily need cycle highways from the city center to the outskirts or universities with people moving quickly, because that can be quite daunting." Just as with children, women, and people with disabilities, planners must ensure that they know where users are and how they use space, to attend to details like street surfaces, resting places, and activity along routes so they will actually want to go outside.

"The relationship between mobility and physical health is not so straightforward," Van Hoven clarifies. "There are many things that impact an older person's mobility, so it's important to provide choices and opportunities for independence." When considering the design and function of a space, we must know who we are prioritizing: the 98 percent that can, for example, use the stairs to access a historical building, or the 2 percent that might visit twice a year. "For me it's about making a statement," says van Hoven. "It's not about 2 percent or 98 percent. It's about whether we want to convey we are an inclusive society. Maybe there will be more than 2 percent if they are able to enter that building."

"I think for a lot of us, when we think about age-friendly neighbourhoods, we think about the house, the street, the shop, but we don't think about the actual practices that take place in these spaces. We attend more to those and what they mean so we can think about enhancing them," says Van Hoven. "The feeling and experience in making these people-friendly cities is not considered as often as a function, and while it is also important, if you are not focusing on feeling and experience you are not going to look for how to enhance it."

In 2007, the World Health Organization published a *Global Age-Friendly Cities* guide identifying eight dimensions an age-friendly city must consider: Outdoor spaces and buildings, transportation, housing, social participation, respect and social inclusion, civic participation and employment, communication and information, community support and health services. "Where is the care, feeling and experience in that?" Van Hoven asks. "You need to make it more explicit, otherwise it remains unseen." She argues that people, regardless of age, crave relevance. "We talk a lot about what the environment can do for aging people, but we've also heard a lot that people want to be meaningful for their environment and for the people in their community." Age-friendly cities need to provide the opportunities that make older adults feel more consequential in their society. Involving them in local projects, even providing opportunities through local networks to pass old trades on to the next generation, can help the elderly feel more connected and relevant to their community.

At a global level, the number of people over the age of 60, which was only 8 percent (200 million people) in 1950, and 11 percent (760 million) in 2011, is expected to reach 22 percent (2 billion) by 2050. But how can we create and enhance the public realm to ensure that aging populations maintain not only their physical activity levels but also their social activity levels? It starts with how we organize the space between buildings, to encourage them to participate in society in a secure and comfortable manner. At the same time, we need to provide ways to allow for meaningful interactions. In communities where many of the elderly people may have actually built the places they live in, what can we do to facilitate inclusion and intergenerational connectivity? "Maybe we should make more effort to discover what people have and how we can use that also in how we think about livable spaces," concludes Van Hoven. "It's not just about what they need but what can they give."

Allowing the Elderly to "CycleOn"

While the idea of having everything within a 500-meter (1,640-feet) radius is an admirable goal, the current reality, even in dense cities, means that residents need to regularly travel outside this bubble. And so, cycling remains an important means of transport for the elderly in the Netherlands, positively contributing to physical and mental health and social inclusion. For many, the bicycle is seen as a "rolling walking stick," a type of mobility device that is far easier on the joints than walking. The high-quality cycling networks across the country mean that a third of trips taken by people aged 65 to 75 are on a bicycle, the highest rate among all adult categories. A 2019 survey by the Universities of Ghent, Brussels, and Utrecht quantified what this means to their travel patterns. It found an elderly Dutch or Belgian person who cycles enjoys a "life sphere" of about 14 kilometers (9 miles) in their daily life. The life sphere of a noncyclist is limited to about 10 kilometers (6 miles).

Electric bikes are offering more and more convenience, allowing older people to remain independently mobile until later and later in life, and making them less dependent on their relatives for transportation. Figures from Statistics Netherlands found that from 2010 to 2017, Dutch seniors 75 and over cycled an average of 33 percent more kilometers. But this increased mobility doesn't come without risk. The same visual impairments and delayed reaction times that affect elderly drivers also affect elderly cyclists, although the latter is largely only a danger to themselves. Of all cycling fatalities across the country in 2019, a disproportionate 59 percent were from this age group, mostly

An elderly person who cycles enjoys a daily "life sphere" of about 14 kilometers (9 miles). The life sphere of a noncyclist is limited to about 10 kilometers (6 miles). (Modacity)

through "one-sided accidents." There is a new push to encourage safer street design and user behavior, beginning with the national government, and working its way down to the municipal level.

Launched by the Ministry of Infrastructure & Water Management in 2019, the Doortrappen (CycleOn) program aims to make elderly cyclists aware of these safety concerns by making the topic open to discussion in places where they already visit, such as community centers and fitness clubs. It is then about compelling them to make adjustments to their bicycle or behavior. Through their own trusted network in the city and at logical moments, cyclists are offered tips, information, and interventions that make them aware of the means they have to improve their own safety. This can be achieved by linking bicycle safety to movement and staying active, by not being patronizing, and by shaping the CycleOn message in a recognizable style, implementing it consistently and continuing to repeat it. The goal? Fewer crashes, greater health benefits, and better quality of life.

Education will get you only so far, however, which is why engineers at local governments are starting to look at their cycling networks through the eyes of the elderly. By widening the infrastructure, removing hazardous bollards, creating more forgiving (i.e., angled) curbs, improving the smoothness of the asphalt, and strengthening the visual lines at the cycleway edges, making the entire network "senior friendly" is the end goal, but one that requires a lot of time, money, and space. In the short term, municipalities, including Amsterdam and Haarlem, have planned several *relaxte routes* (relaxed routes)—marked by yellow hearts—and promotes them to older cyclists as low-traffic, low-stress, more-forgiving alternatives.

In a nation of cyclists, these steps are designed to maintain and possibly increase cycling rates among seniors. At the same time, much of the infrastructure networks and car management policies create space both for walking and also for people using mobility aids. As Dr. Van Hoven noted, these measures don't just make cities age friendly, they make them people friendly; places where everyone regardless of age, ability, or activity can travel through and also stop and rest, and maybe connect with someone new while they're at it.

Staying Active as Long as the Body—and Mind—Will Allow

Spending a lifetime walking and cycling on Delft's streets and teaching in its schools, Peter has, without intention, created a vast network of family, friends, and social acquaintances. Whether he wants to or not, nearly every venture outside his home includes "stop-and-chats." He revels in these opportunities that, as it turns out, are not confined to city limits. As an avid traveler, he has spent many months visiting faraway countries, and so have his former students. "It seems each time I'm out I bump into someone I know. Even on a beach in Mexico, on the island of Sri Lanka, or in a train in China! It's unbelievable," he muses.

Just as working with students fulfills his desire to keep his brain working, traveling and learning about other cultures has always fascinated Peter. Even now, when he can't fly quite as far as he may have in his younger years, he continues his learning through television programming, often having National Geographic programs on in the background. "I like to meet other cultures and to learn about them," he says. "Meeting people, teaching the students, watching TV—especially traveling programs—keeps the mind active."

Of course, walking and cycling everywhere keeps Peter's body active as well. But he feels quite fortunate to be able to maintain his mobility. A few years earlier, that ability to travel independently came under threat. After starting to experience some discomfort and stiffness in his joints, a doctor's diagnosis revealed that he had developed rheumatoid arthritis. "I thought, 'What's going to happen with me now?'" he recalls. Immediately he started thinking about having to install a lift on his stairs to adapt them to his changing needs, and other ways he might have to adjust the home he had built in the neighborhood he had grown up in. "But I didn't see myself sitting in a wheelchair," Peter admits. "It became very hard; I didn't want to live that kind of dependent life." He praises the wonders of modern medicine for helping him return to his normal mobility levels. All it took was three small pills once per week, and over time the pain disappeared: "I noticed it wasn't getting worse, and then eventually it got better and I was able to continue living independently."

The situation did begin a new conversation for Peter and his sibling. "I hope to stay in this area for as long as I am physically able to," he emphasizes, "but when it is my time, and I can no longer be independent, I want the choice of whether to continue living or not." In the Netherlands, euthanasia is permissible through a written directive from a patient and consultation with and assistance by their doctor. "These are questions you think about as you get older," Peter says quite directly. He has also discussed the options with Chris, understanding that as his dementia worsens over time, the level of care Peter, their brothers, and family and friends can provide will be insufficient. For both of them, the ability to stay and age in place as long as their minds and bodies will allow is paramount. For now, the routine of walking to the store and seeing friendly faces helps, but over time, they want to live comfortably, and if they cannot, then they will say, "I'm finished."

Until then, Peter's feet seldom hit the ground. From meeting with friends in town, helping local students, and even cleaning the footpaths

Chris's retired parents riding a *duofiets* (duo bike) during a 2019 visit to Delft. Build space for cycling and calm the traffic in your city, and that's when the magic happens. (Modacity)

on our street, these activities ensure that he remains connected with his community. "It's better for your way of living," he states, "I just have too much energy!" Peter admits that he only enjoys cycling with a destination in mind, so it's unlikely we'll bump into him on one of our recreational rides. But he does enjoy excursions that give cycling a purpose. In the summer of 2019, together with Chris, our neighbor Marieke, his nephew and a friend, they coordinated a cycle trip to Valkenburg, a small town just east of Maastricht in the Province of Limburg. There they stayed at a local hotel, traveling around by e-bike in the countryside. With the hotel as their "home base," and the boost of the electric bikes to flatten the hills of Limburg, Peter was able to fulfill his desire to travel while also being with Chris, who, in his condition, can no longer hop on a plane and visit the faraway places they used to go. "It was very pleasant, and we plan to do it again in the years to come, so long as someone else will plan it for me," he laughs.

This unique sense of community we found on our street and observed among our neighbors, and within the larger city of Delft, has made us really appreciate what it means to live in an age-friendly city. It's a place where our children can meet people like Peter and Marieke, and make social contacts beyond their peers, where we feel a part of a larger group, even as outsiders still learning the language, who are valued and important members of our community. We feel very lucky to have happened upon this gem of a place, and can easily picture ourselves wandering its streets in our twilight years, passing familiar faces, and being able to happily age in place, as long as our minds and bodies will allow.

Exporting the "Low-Car" City

I t's now August 2020, exactly four years since we completed our first Dutch adventure as a family, and a year and a half after landing in Delft to start a new life as *buitenlanders* (foreigners) in the Netherlands. These types of adventures are never easy or straightforward: we left many close friends and family behind in Canada, and fully immersed ourselves in a new culture, forcing each of us to learn a new language and discover our own way in the process. Anyone who has made a move such as this will tell you it is impossible to anticipate the outcome, how it may change who you understand yourself to be, and how truly difficult it is. Because social media makes it look easy—to our loved ones back in Canada, it likely appears as though we've comfortably landed in the city/careers/lives of our dreams. But we will be the first to admit that the uprooting of our relatively comfortable lives in Vancouver has come with plenty of struggles, tears, and homesickness.

Now, 18 months later and despite the challenges, we know it was worth it. A "lightbulb moment" occurred for all of us as we cycled along the rural paths in the province of Drenthe. It was the return journey after a week of summer camp for Etienne. As always, Mom and Dad said, "We couldn't do this in Vancouver." But Coralie, now 14, was moaning about the discomfort of her saddle after 18 kilometers (11 miles) of cycling, when she suddenly announced, "This is really amazing to be able to do this." We had passed through forests, endless fields and pastures, and plenty of farm life. All the while, we were completely separated from cars on nearly every route, and what cars we did encounter were few and far between. Despite the length of the journey, and a headwind that seemed to change direction every time we did, the scale of such a trip and the incredible privilege of the experience were not lost on our teen.

During our lengthy strolls through Delft, we are always aware that the life we now enjoy is an immense privilege. But it shouldn't be. Thinking back to where we grew up in southern Ontario, we recollect being able to walk and cycle more. We also remember those human-powered trips disappearing through our teenage years as streets became busier and busier with car traffic. We remember the historic downtown of Guelph, Ontario, and how smitten we were with that city, but how we also felt resigned to automobile ownership because we simply couldn't navigate the city's large arterials on two wheels. And we recall living through the transformations in Vancouver that took us from simply being people who used a bike to becoming advocates for calmer, more people friendly places. In each of these periods of our lives, one constant has remained: the increasing dominance of motor vehicles on the streets.

Experiencing the Netherlands not just as tourists but as residents has shown us the necessity and urgency of exporting this way of life around the world—even more than the emotions that inspired us to write *Building the Cycling City*. Sure, the Dutch have had a five-decade head start, but that means they've shown what is possible if decision makers take risks and put people first. When they do so, they create places where children experience the freedom many experts say has been lost in the face of technology, overscheduling, and hyperparenting. And they create places where residents across age, race, physical ability, and economic status share space more equitably, safely, and comfortably.

The fact remains that benefits such as childhood autonomy, social connectivity, economic equity, and the ability to age in place were generally not stated outcomes of these "traffic evaporation" policies. The social, emotional, and psychological impacts we have experienced in moving to Delft are unanticipated by-products of transportation policies that were aimed at reducing the dominance of cars on its streets. Traffic circulation plans, network-based design policies, traffic-calming measures, and the supply of multimodal connectedness all combine to create spaces where people can metaphorically and literally "breathe."

The wonderful reality is that, just as cities can learn from the Dutch how to build toward urban vitality, the same can be said for these less-transport-focused ideals. Since 2016, Barcelona (population 5.6 million) has been rolling out its transformational "Superblocks" scheme, which restricts through traffic to every ninth street, and opens up entire neighborhoods to pedestrians, cyclists, and playing children. In the heart of Texas, the City of Austin (population 2.2 million) is midway through the construction of a comprehensive 354-kilometer (220-mile), $150 million bicycle network, informed and inspired by the Dutch approach. And in March 2020, Auckland, New Zealand (population 1.6 million), passed an ambitious traffic circulation plan entitled Access for Everyone, which pedestrianizes large parts of its core, and restricts through traffic in the surrounding precincts. After decades of ignoring the successes of its neighbor across the North Sea, the United Kingdom is finally "going Dutch," with the opening of the nation's first fully protected intersection (in Manchester, population 510,000) and Dutch-style roundabout (in Cambridge, population 124,000) in the summer of 2020.

While many of the qualitative benefits we've presented were not policy driven, for cities outside the Netherlands to achieve similar success, they must be. Not only by creating design and planning guidelines, but by explicitly stating that access to transport, gender and racial equity, mobility for people of all ages and for those with disabilities, and the provision of natural, green spaces are all basic human rights.

The fading of gender mainstreaming in European planning is proof that unless it is written into permanent policy, these "nice ideas" will often be either overlooked or scrapped when budgets are cut, or new priorities are presented in their place.

We feel quite lucky to have had this opportunity, and often believe that we've stumbled on a secret many other cities haven't been told yet. Visitors to the Netherlands often say that you can't truly understand what it is that you're missing until you come here. Author Pete Jordan so succinctly described it when he recounted stepping out of Amsterdam Centraal and feeling like he was hearing again for the first time. We would have agreed that, yes, you need to come here and experience the quiet, the trust, the safety, and the comfort, in order to understand why it is so critical to export these ideas across the globe. That is, until March 2020.

At the start of the COVID-19 crisis, cities around the world suddenly fell silent; or at least car-silent. For the first time in a generation, people in countless places experienced what most Dutch people encounter every day. The quiet that comes when a city goes *autoluw* (low-car or nearly car-free), and the social activity stimulated when you are empowered to walk or cycle through your neighborhood, enjoying fresh air and opportunities for physical activity. We remember a post from our friend Clarence Eckerson Jr. sitting in the middle of a major Manhattan intersection, and saying he could hear birds chirping in the heart of New York City for the first time in his life. The "city that never sleeps" was sleeping, or at least its cars were.

As lockdown led to a potential rise in depression, loneliness, and anxiety, the city streets became the place where residents could escape and feel a part of their community again—even at a distance. The needs for physical distancing due to COVID-19 presented the opportunity for both residents and city leaders to reexamine how to allocate public space. Large cities, such as New York, Paris, Berlin, and Vancouver, created pop-up bike lanes, extended sidewalks and patios, and established low-traffic streets, all in an effort to make the experience of walking or cycling safer. Even smaller cities, including our former home of Guelph—which created a "Dining District" in its temporarily car-free center—implemented measures to improve the comfort of citizens and the viability of small businesses. While the circumstances around these developments have been an absolute tragedy for countless people, these transformations happened without too much fuss, and eventually, with celebration. In nearly every case, the temporary measures were part of long-term plans that already existed prior to the pandemic, but their execution was accelerated in response. If anything, the quick response is proof that these changes don't need to be part of lofty 25- and 50-year plans. With sufficient political will, and demand from the public, cities can change almost overnight.

In an age of constant activity, where we're all so busy that we take vacations specifically designed to "unplug" from the world and "escape" the insanity of being constantly on the go, what has struck us most is the way our new home creates those opportunities just by us stepping outside our front door. Peter told us that he likes talking to everyone, even strangers in an elevator. But we have come to notice that his behavior is not the exception. In a nation accustomed to engaging in social mobility on a regular basis, it is rare that people *don't* say "hallo" as we pass on the street, or smile when one yields to another. Whether it be with a neighbor or a stranger, the levels of connection we experience in Delft are reminiscent of those we would only experience in cottage country in Canada. Who's to say, though, that this kind of experience can't happen in every community, of any size, in any city. Research has proven that social, and, more importantly physical, interaction is so integral not just to our feelings of happiness but to our overall health. City staff can't make friends for us, but they can create streets and public spaces in our cities that increase the opportunity to meet our fellow citizens and form meaningful relationships.

When we first sat down to write this book, we wanted to communicate to the world what we had been experiencing in Delft. We hoped that our words would inspire change. The fact that everyone has encountered exactly what we were sharing via social media, and through the stories in this book, at first made us question whether these pages were even necessary. Now we recognize that everyone living, even briefly, in a world that resembles what we enjoy in our daily lives should offer support to the argument of creating "low-car" cities everywhere.

In the years and decades to come, the fragility of our social, economic, and transportation systems will be tested with increasing frequency and amplitude. The climate crisis is no longer a looming possibility, it is a present reality. Each year, weather extremes get worse and worse. Resiliency in the face of these catastrophic disasters will be what determines which cities survive and which struggle to overcome them. The COVID-19 pandemic is proof that these dangers are universal, and by learning from one another, adapting and evolving from previously established norms will be the keys to our survival. The Netherlands is not perfect, nor is it immune to the challenges ahead. But because of a confluence of events that started before we were born, this entire country—including small cities like Delft—has placed itself in a position where much of the necessary diversity and flexibility is already built into the urban fabric and can be adjusted when circumstances demand it.

After landing on Dutch soil in the summer of 2016, we knew within days that we would do everything in our power to relocate our family from Canada. Sure, it may have begun with an ability to cycle everywhere without stress, but in those five weeks, we knew if we wanted our children to grow up where they could be "free range." And if the two of us wanted to age comfortably in a place that made us feel as welcome as our younger counterparts, moving to the Netherlands wasn't an option, it was an imperative. But we never could have anticipated the swift changes to our physical and emotional health, and we are still discovering new benefits this new life brings with it. But when we reflect, it feels like we were always meant to be here.

We liked Guelph because of the quaint, "small town" vibe. We liked Vancouver because we could travel on foot or bicycle in a built environment that blended well with the natural environment. Delft may not have mountains or ocean, but here, we have the perfect combination of small, but connected urban life. We enjoy close proximity to nature while maintaining access to the cultural benefits of the nearby big cities; all reachable by foot, bike, or public transport. Everyone dreams of finding a place they don't feel the need to escape from.

We have found ours in Delft. But we know that, by looking back through its journey, what has been achieved here is not unique. Delft

The perfect ending to our family's Dutch fairytale: in November 2020, we bought a 130-year-old *grachtenpand* (canal house) on the silent (i.e., totally car-free) side of a Delft canal. (Modacity)

shows us what is possible when we reduce the supremacy of motor vehicles from our lives and prioritize the human experience. With the right leadership, traffic evaporation policies, as well as those aimed at improving social connection, reducing noise, addressing mental health and equity, and ensuring resiliency regardless of what environmental and health challenges are yet to come, cities of all sizes can provide the quality of life our family now cherishes. We understand *why* it is so important to have fewer cars in our lives. The critical next step starts today. Now is the time to make it happen.

About the Authors

Melissa and Chris Bruntlett are Canadian authors and urban mobility advocates who strive to communicate the benefits of sustainable transport and inspire happier, healthier, more human-scale cities. Their first book, *Building the Cycling City: The Dutch Blueprint for Urban Vitality*, explored the urban and transport planning decisions that established the Netherlands as a bicycle paradise, and how North American communities are translating these ideas to build their own cycling cities.

In 2019, Melissa and Chris, along with their children Coralie and Etienne, relocated from Vancouver, Canada, to Delft, the Netherlands. Melissa now works with Mobycon—a bicontinental mobility consultancy—supporting the promotion of Dutch transport knowledge, policy, and design principles in countries across Europe and North America. As communications manager for the Dutch Cycling Embassy, Chris uses his knowledge and passion to share practical lessons for global cities wishing to learn from the Netherlands' extraordinary success. Together they continue to be inspired by their new home, watching their children (and countless others) enjoy a quality of life only possible in an environment that puts people first.

Acknowledgments

Writing this book has been a labor of love, challenging us to look outside our usual mobility circles to the greater impacts of car-dominant mobility. This would not have been possible without the countless people who offered insight, knowledge, and support throughout the process.

First, a big thank you to Mirjam Borsboom and Johan Diepens who recognized the potential of these two Canadians, offering us the jobs that would enable us to follow our dreams to the Netherlands. The themes that inspired this book would not have been possible without your initial support.

Thanks to Heather Boyer, our editor, and the entire Island Press team for continuing to allow us to share our stories with audiences around the world.

Learning about the history of Delft's policies and planning decisions was made possible with the generous help of Gemeente Delft staff Jan Nederveen and Jan-Kees Verrest, and former staff member André Pettinga.

Communicating the importance of the themes explored in this book would not have been achieved without all of the experts who generously took the time to sit down with us for an interview, especially at a time when we were all spending our days on never-ending online calls and meetings: Dr. Lia Karsten, Dr. Bruce Appleyard, Dr. Marco te Brömmelstroet, Katrina Johnston-Zimmerman, Dr. Edda Bild, Dr. Robin Mazumder, Dr. Bridget Burdett, Jeroen Bastiaanssen, Dr. Judith (Y. T.) Yang, and Dr. Bettina van Hoven.

We are also truly grateful to the individuals who shared their personal stories of life in Delft with us: Maya van der Does-Levi for helping us better understand what freedoms can be enjoyed when living with a disability, and Peter de Kat for sharing your stories of a happy, long life spent on Delft's cozy streets.

Special thanks to our colleagues and friends who generously offered their time to review a draft of our manuscript, ultimately creating a better book for it: Mark Ames, Lucas Harms, Sarah Marchionda, Mark Ostrow, and Kay Teschke.

Finally, deepest thanks to our extraordinary children who continue to challenge how we see the world around us and keep motivating us to fight the good fight. Your patience with parents who never seem to stop working, and your resilience in adapting to a new country, language, and culture, are truly inspiring. We couldn't be prouder of the amazing humans you are becoming!

Bibliography

Alter, Lloyd. "The 15-Minute City Is Having a Moment." Accessed July 28, 2020. https://www.treehugger.com/the-15-minute-city-is-having-a-moment-5071739/.

Alter, Lloyd. "To Fight Climate Change, We Need to Get More Women on Bikes." Accessed September 4, 2020. https://www.treehugger.com/fight-climate-change-we-need-get-more-women-bikes-4852688.

"The Ageing Population: Numbers and Statistics." Accessed July 28, 2020. http://www.silvereco.org/en/statistics/.

Aldred, Rachel, and James Woodcock. "Transport: Challenging Disabling Environments." *International Journal of Justice and Sustainability*, 2008.

Appleyard, Bruce. "The Meaning of Livable Streets to Schoolchildren: An Image Mapping Study of the Effects of Traffic on Children's Cognitive Development of Spatial Knowledge." *Journal of Transport & Health*, 2016.

Appleyard, Donald, and Mark Lintell. *Environmental Quality of City Streets: The Residents' Viewpoint*. Highway Research Record, 1971.

Biddulph, Mike. "Street Design and Street Use: Comparing Traffic Calmed and Home Zone Streets." *Journal of Urban Design*, 2012.

"Boids." Accessed April 26, 2020. https://en.wikipedia.org/wiki/Boids.

Bouchard, Mikayla. "Transportation Emerges as Crucial to Escaping Poverty." Accessed July 5, 2020. https://www.nytimes.com/2015/05/07/upshot/transportation-emerges-as-crucial-to-escaping-poverty.html.

Bowdler, Janis, et al. *Building Equitable Cities: How to Drive Economic Mobility and Regional Growth*. Urban Land Institute, 2017.

Bruntlett, Melissa. "Good Speed by Design: A Network Approach to Traffic Calming." Accessed April 13, 2020. https://mobycon.com/updates/good-speed-by-design-a-network-approach-to-traffic-calming/.

Buchholz, Katharina. "Americans Now Spend Less Than 8 Percent of Their Time Outdoors." Accessed June 6, 2020. https://www.statista.com/chart/21408/time-americans-spend-indoors-outdoors/.

Buffel, Tine, Sophie Handler, and Chris Phillipson. *Age-Friendly Cities and Communities: A Global Perspective*. Policy Press, 2019.

Carrington, Damian. "Car Tyres Are Major Source of Ocean Microplastics—Study." Accessed July 21, 2020. https://www.theguardian.com/environment/2020/jul/14/car-tyres-are-major-source-of-ocean-microplastics-study/.

Chaput, Jean-Philippe, Caroline Dutil, and Hugues Sampasa-Kanyinga. "Sleeping Hours: What Is the Ideal Number and How Does Age Impact This?" *Nature and Science of Sleep*, 2018.

Collarte, Natalia. *The Woonerf Concept: Rethinking a Residential Street in Somerville*. Tufts University, 2012.

Colley, R. C., et al. *Physical Activity of Canadian Children and Youth: Accelerometer Data from the 2007 to 2009 Canadian Health Measures Survey.* Statistics Canada, 2011.

Cortright, Joe. "Less in Common." Accessed September 4, 2020. https://cityobserv atory.org/wp-content/uploads/2015/06/CityObservatory_Less_In_Common.pdf.

Cross, R. J., and Tony Dutzik. "Driving into Debt: The Hidden Costs of Risky Auto Loans to Consumers and Our Communities." Accessed July 15, 2020. https://us pirg.org/feature/usp/driving-debt/.

Den Boer, Eelco, and Arno Schroten. *Traffic Noise Reduction in Europe: Health Effects, Social Costs, and Technical and Policy Options to Reduce Road and Rail Traffic Noise.* CE Delft, 2007.

Doane, Leah, and E. K. Adam. "Loneliness and Cortisol: Momentary, Day-to-Day, and Trait Associations." *Psychoneuroendocrinology*, 2010.

"Effect and Function of Green Tracks." Accessed July 21, 2020. http://www.gruengleis netzwerk.de/images/downloads/effects.pdf.

Eulalia, Peris. *Noise Pollution Is a Major Problem, Both for Human Health and the Environment.* European Environmental Agency, 2020.

Fleerackers, Alice. "The Simple Dutch Cure for Stress." Accessed June 6, 2020. http:// nautil.us/blog/the-simple-dutch-cure-for-stress/.

Fleming, Stephen. "Green Maps." Accessed March 27, 2020. https://cycle-space.com /green-maps/.

Frazer, Lance. "Paving Paradise: The Peril of Impervious Surfaces." *Environmental Health Perspectives*, 2005.

Friedman, Aaron, Aaron Naparstek, and Mateo Taussig-Rubbo. "Alarmingly Useless: The Case for Banning Car Alarms in New York City." Accessed May 15, 2020. https://www.transalt.org/sites/default/files/news/reports/2003/Alarmingly _Useless.pdf.

Goodyear, Sarah. "The Link between Kids Who Walk or Bike to School and Con-centration." Accessed April 3, 2020. https://www.citylab.com/transportation/2013 /02/kids-who-walk-or-bike-school-concentrate-better-study-shows/4585/.

Griggs, Mary Beth. "Birds Are Changing Their Songs to Shout Over Traffic Noise." Accessed May 15, 2020. https://www.popsci.com/birds-traffic-noise/.

Halpern, David. "Social Trust Is One of the Most Important Measures That Most People Have Never Heard of—and It's Moving." Accessed April 26, 2020. https:// www.bi.team/blogs/social-trust-is-one-of-the-most-important-measures-that -most-people-have-never-heard-of-and-its-moving/.

"The High Cost of Transportation in the United States." Accessed July 5, 2020. https:// www.itdp.org/2019/05/23/high-cost-transportation-united-states/.

"How Does Social Isolation Affect a Child's Mental Health and Development?" Accessed March 27, 2020. https://www.noisolation.com/global/research/how-does -social-isolation-affect-a-childs-mental-health-and-development/.

"How Urban Design Affects Mental Health." Accessed June 6, 2020. https://www.cbc .ca/radio/thesundayedition/the-sunday-edition-for-february-16-2020-1.5459411 /how-urban-design-affects-mental-health-1.5462455/.

Huffman, John Pearley. "Hurricane Harvey Destroyed More Vehicles Than Any Single Event in America. This Is the Aftermath." Accessed July 30, 2020. https://

www.caranddriver.com/features/a18370403/hurricane-harvey-destroyed-more
-vehicles-than-any-single-event-in-america-this-is-the-aftermath-feature/.

Imrie, Rob. *Disability and the City: International Perspectives*. Paul Chapman Publishing, 1996.

Karsten, Lia. "It All Used to Be Better? Different Generations on Continuity and Change in Urban Children's Daily Use of Space." *Children's Geographies*, 2005.

Karsten, Lia. *On Childhoods and Cities or the Changing Relationship between the Street, the School and Children's Consumption Spaces*. Uppsala University, 2013.

Lucas, Karen, et al. *Inequalities in Mobility and Access in the UK Transport System*. Government Office for Science, 2019.

Lundberg, Kent. "Wijkontsluitingsweg." Accessed March 27, 2020. https://www.great erauckland.org.nz/2017/08/15/wijkontsluitingsweg/.

Marsh, Calum. "Is Honking a Crisis? How One Simple Safety Measure Has Grown into an Audible Scourge for the Urban-Dweller." Accessed May 15, 2020. https://nationalpost.com/entertainment/is-honking-a-crisis-how-one-simple-safety -measure-has-grown-into-an-audible-scourge-for-the-urban-dweller.

"Mental Health Facts in America." Accessed June 6, 2020. https://ibcces.org/blog/2019/04/09/mental-health-training-gap-schools/mental-health-facts-in -america-mental-health-crisis-numbers-nami/.

Montgomery, Charles. *Happy City: Transforming Our Lives through Urban Design*. Farrar, Straus and Giroux, 2013.

National Academy of Sciences. "Social Isolation and Loneliness in Older Adults." Accessed April 21, 2020. https://www.nap.edu/catalog/25663/social-isolation-and -loneliness-in-older-adults-opportunities-for-the.

Newman, Peter, Timothy Beatley, and Heather Boyer. *Resilient Cities: Overcoming Fossil Fuel Dependence*. Island Press, 2017.

Ozdenerol, Esra, et al. "The Impact of Traffic Noise on Housing Values." *Journal of Real Estate Practice and Education*, 2015.

Pinker, Susan. *The Village Effect: Why Face-to-Face Contact Matters*. Vintage Books, 2015.

Polycarpou, Lakis. "No More Pavement! The Problem of Impervious Surfaces." Accessed July 21, 2020. https://blogs.ei.columbia.edu/2010/07/13/no-more-pave ment-the-problem-of-impervious-surfaces/.

Rider, David. "How the Gardiner Expressway Hogs the Road during Budget Talks." Accessed July 12, 2020. https://www.thestar.com/news/city_hall/2020/02/10/how-the-gardiner-expressway-hogs-the-road-during-budget-talks.html.

Sánchez de Madariaga, Inés, and Marion Roberts. *Fair Shared Cities: The Impact of Gender Planning in Europe*. Routledge, 2016.

Schepel, Steven. "Woonerf Revisited: Delft as an Example." Accessed April 13, 2020. http://www.woonerfgoed.nl/int/Childstreet_files/StevenSchepel.pdf.

Sennett, Richard. *Together: The Rituals, Pleasures and Politics of Cooperation*. Yale University Press, 2013.

Skenazy, Lenore. *Free-Range Kids: How to Raise Safe, Self-Reliant Children (Without Going Nuts with Worry)*. Jossey-Bass, 2009.

"Statistics on Road Safety and Elderly Drivers." Accessed July 30, 2020. https://

www.3m.com/3M/en_US/road-safety-us/resources/road-transportation
-safety-center-blog/full-story/~/statistics-on-elderly-drivers/?storyid=69b6d08e-f44e
-4538-b2bb-322a7de3f9of.

Steinberg, Lior. "It's the Design Guide, Stupid—American vs. Dutch Cycling Infrastructure." Accessed July 3, 2020. https://www.humankind.city/post/it-s-the -design-guide-stupid-american-vs-dutch-cycling-infrastructure.

Stewart, John, et al. *Why Noise Matters: A Worldwide Perspective on the Problems, Policies and Solutions.* Taylor & Francis, 2011.

Te Brömmelstroet, Marco, et al. "Travelling Together Alone and Alone Together: Mobility and Potential Exposure to Diversity." *Applied Mobilities*, 2017.

Tumlin, Jeff. "Sex, Neuroscience and Walkable Urbanism." Accessed April 17, 2020. https://www.youtube.com/watch?v=WHet2jjHtk4.

Turley Voulgaris, Carole, Michael Smart, and Brian Taylor. "Tired of Commuting? Relationships among Journeys to School, Sleep, and Exercise among American Teenagers." *Journal of Planning Education and Research*, 2017.

Vanderbilt, Tom. *Traffic: Why We Drive the Way We Do (and What It Says about Us).* Knopf, Borzoi Books, 2008.

Wagenbuur, Mark. "The 1979 Delft Cycle Plan." Accessed May 22, 2020. https://bi cycledutch.wordpress.com/2019/02/27/the-1979-delft-cycle-plan/.

Wagenbuur, Mark. "Bicycle Parking at Delft Central Station." Accessed July 15, 2020. https://bicycledutch.wordpress.com/2015/06/02/bicycle-parking-at-delft-central -station/.

Wang, Judith Y. T. "'Resilience Thinking' in Transport Planning." *Civil Engineering and Environmental Systems*, 2015.

Weetman, Robert. "What Nobody Told Me. . . ." Accessed July 30, 2020. https:// robertweetman.wordpress.com/2017/10/12/what-nobody-told-me-1/.